ADVENTURE
PHILANTHROPIST

Great Adventures Volunteering Abroad

Erin Michelson

ISBN: 978-0-9910016-0-6 (sc)
ISBN: 978-0-9910016-1-3 (e)

Ordering Information:
Bookstores and wholesalers contact the publisher via email: Info@GoErinGo.com. Special discounts are available on quantity purchases by retail establishments, corporations, educators, and associations.

Published by emCom LLC: November 7, 2013

For Dad: C2C

Contents

Photos & Videos

More than 200 photos and 70 videos illustrating each chapter of the book can be found on www.GoErinGo.com.

Group Reading Guide

Questions and discussion topics for book clubs are located on www.GoErinGo.com.

Acknowledgements

When we strike out on an adventure, we never truly travel alone. Instead there is a bevy of supporters who walk beside us. I'd like acknowledge my friends and family who joined me on the writing leg of this journey.

Thanks Sam! My mom Sam is my favorite travel buddy. She met me twice during my two-year odyssey, once in Europe and once to tour South Asia. Sam was supportive of my idea from the start, standing in my corner lending both sage advice and motherly concern. A mother-daughter relationship like ours is rare and I treasure it every day.

Thanks Lucy! Lucy Walker was my first reader. A former editor at Random House, Lucy and I were tent mates during an overland trucking tour of Southern Africa. Lucy was the first person to read my initial chapters and she gave me incredibly helpful feedback and advice. Even more important, she gave me unbridled encouragement at this tender stage in my writing.

Thanks Susan! Susan Power is my editor. We met on a beach in Sri Lanka, but it was while visiting her in Brighton that I learned that she was a freelance editor. Her deft comments during the pre-read convinced me that she was the editor for me—and I was right! I have no doubt that this book is better because of her insights and tactful input.

Thanks Pre-Readers! With the introduction and two chapters in hand, I asked a boatful of friends if they would provide early feedback. To my surprise, twenty-three of you did! I so appreciate the thoughtful comments and kind notes of support from all my pre-readers:

> Barbara Butcher, Moira Jean Byers, Kristina Caratan, Dawn Cole, Liz Coryell, Ken & Jerry Cottrell, Angelina Edward, Cherie Jardine O'Connor, Ryann Johnson, Hilde Löfqvist, Machie Madden, Sam Michelson, Sonal Patel, Susan Power, Lori Sackman, Dorothy Salmon, Natasha Shulman, Althea Stevens, Vanessa Stimac, Rizwan Tayabali, Julie Walker, Lucy Walker

Thanks Kickstarter Supporters! Kickstarter is a way for entrepreneurs to raise money for creative projects. To help me publish this book, I ran a crowd-funding campaign where I asked my mates to match my initial investment of $6,000. More than 80 of you chipped in—to the tune of $6,773! I am grateful for your generosity and faith in my ability to finish the book:

> Marek Alboszta, Brigitte Amiri, Katherine Auld, Laura Barrera, Anne Benoist, Jennifer Benton, Antoinette Bernardo, Clara Beshoar, Kimmy Bettinger, Beverly Bronson, Heather Brown, Ryan J. Burke, Moira Jean Byers, Kristina Caratan, Laura Carroll, Nancy Chellevold, Dawn Cole, Deirdre Combs, Stacy Cooper Dent, Liz Coryell, Adam Cox, Lourdes Davila, Pamela Day, Elaine Dermondy, Vania Dimova, Roxanne Dowell,

Angelina Edwards, Lisa Flanagan, Jen Gaarder-Wang, Erin S. Gore, Karoline Graeubig, Ryan Higgins, Paul Hodge, Leonard Hoops, Annie Irving, Harriet Israel, Nancy L. Janke, Cherie Jardine O'Connor, Lauane Jetty, Catherine Karnow, Chris Klug, Sherazade Langlade, Jane Levikow, Hilde Löfqvist, Brenda Logan, Laura Marshall, Oona Marti, Joan Michelson, Sam Michelson, Linda N. Michelson, Jeff Michie, Barbara Minch-Rosenberg, Patty Mok, Mary Ann Montano, Greg Nelson, Courtney Oliva, Keir Oxley, Rick Passo, Sonal Patel, Susan Pease, Simon Pierce, Marianna Pisano, Teresa Qu, Cathy Rafii, Josh Riedel, Laurie Rud, Carol Rumpf, Hector Sanchez, Aarti Shah, Natasha Shulman, Teresa Simmermacher, Tarah Smith Evans, Jodi Soboll, Lenelle Suliguin, Rizwan Tayabali, Leslie Theodore, Paula Vance, Melissa Villa, Rasa Vitalia, Lucy Walker, Heidi Young

I'd also like to thank my Kickstarter crew who came together within a week to make my online campaign possible: producer Laurie Rud, film editor Stephanie Dawson, and illustrator and book cover designer Kristopher Fillon. You guys rock!

Thank You! A heartfelt thanks to you, reader, for choosing to read *Adventure Philanthropist*. I appreciate the constraints on everyone's time these days and your decision to spend several hours taking this adventure is thrilling. Thank you for joining me on this journey!

Introduction

Hi, my name is Erin, and I'm an Adventure Philanthropist.

What I really am is someone who is curious about the world, with a thirst for adventure and exploring the unknown. I love learning about new communities and meeting interesting people. And I want to lead a more purposeful, personally fulfilling life. That's why I decided to spend two years travelling around the world, volunteering with local organizations along the way and having a whole lot of fun. There were plenty of adventures, some of them heartening, some of them harrowing, many are found in this book.

I became an Adventure Philanthropist by accident. I had just quit a loathsome job in the corporate world and decided to escape to Africa for a few months. I went white water rafting on the Nile River, I climbed Mt. Kilimanjaro, scuba dived in Zanzibar, and trekked the Usambara Mountains.

It was an incident here in the mountains of central Tanzania that set me thinking. I was staying in the town of Lushoto, when a group of fellow travellers and I visited the Mpanga Primary School, serving students between the ages of seven and fourteen.

In preparation for our visit, we went on a shopping expedition to buy some gifts for the children. Tito, our local guide, suggested that we buy paper, pencils, chalk—basic necessities for the school. But we collectively rejected Tito's advice (school supplies seemed so boring) and instead bought an assortment of sports equipment, musical instruments, and art supplies. Much more fun!

We arrived at Mpanga Primary and met the school principal in his office. When we presented our gifts, he thanked us profusely, telling us that the sports equipment and art supplies would make school more enjoyable and help encourage the kids to attend.

He then took us on a tour of the classrooms and we discovered that the children go to school in shifts, due to lack of space. Even so, they still sat squeezed six to a desk, sharing one book. Some classrooms had more than a hundred students in them. Groups of students sat on the floor.

Seeing the condition of the school made us tourists take a step back. It became crystal clear that we had selfishly bought the children what we wanted them to have, not what they needed. Here the students didn't have any paper for their assignments and few books, and we had given them playthings. We were the ones learning the lesson that day.

For their part, the students were excited to meet a group of foreign visitors and honoured us by lining up outside the school to sing and dance for us in the African tradition. Next it was our turn to sing and dance. Our group of international travellers chose the one song that most of us knew—the chicken dance—which we had practiced the night before.

We got up in front of the students and quacked with our hands, flapped our wings, and shook our tail feathers (more or less in unison). We pulled a couple of students from the audience to join us and the kids were beside themselves with laugher. Several fell to the ground in hysterics, especially when the principal got up to shake his rear-end too.

Afterwards, a couple of us decided to make a group donation to the school, which our tour company handsomely matched. Jointly we were able to raise $800 towards the purchase of building supplies to make twenty new desks and give those kids more room to learn. How great was that!

The new desks were a much better use of funds than the flutes and paints we originally bought. That said, the kids loved the soccer ball, which replaced a ball of rags they had been kicking around. Can you imagine: 750 kids sharing one ball of rags?

Meeting these children was the highlight of my first trip to East Africa. Their commitment and sense of fun made me realize what my travels could offer beyond simple enjoyment: personal enrichment, political edification, a more profound understanding of humanity. Pretty heady stuff.

This insight offered me an enormous opportunity to grow as an individual. To my mind, I had been given a prized gift. And part of what I learned is that I could give a gift in return.

This trip to the Usambara planted a seed in my life. I was at a crossroads in my career and had been planning to launch a consulting firm. I still did this, but with a new-found focus. I arranged my contracts so I could travel overseas at least three months a year. During these trips, I was able to spend time volunteering with local communities.

My life was no longer about solely building a business back home. It was about building a life across the globe. Little did I know where this would take me.

The Adventure Begins

After running my consulting firm for several years that seed grew and blossomed into an irresistible idea. After my most successful year as a consultant, I decided to use the money I was saving to buy a house to fund a two-year trip exploring the world. In addition, I sold all my possessions to start a charitable giving fund so I could make donations along the way. I was all-in.

See, I'm not a trust-fund baby. Those were hard choices I made. That said, I'm grateful for the advantages I had growing up in a loving middle-class home and for the opportunity to attend college. From an early age my parents introduced me to international travel, giving me a taste for adventure that is never quite sated. I'm always ready to pack up and head overseas, explore new locales, sample foreign foods, and experience fascinating cultures first hand.

So the idea of volunteering as I travelled made great sense. It was a way to delve even deeper into a culture, to connect with people, and make new friends. It turned out to be all that—and so much more.

Before I set off, I started my blog: www.GoErinGo.com. It was a way for me to report back in real time what I was experiencing while living my life on the road. Sharing what I learned about world issues and fostering a dialogue was a crucial part of my journey towards being an Adventure Philanthropist.

One of the most important features of the blog became the Donate My Dollars poll. Nearly every month I launch a poll and readers of GoErinGo.com vote on which projects we should support and how much I should give to each organization. My objective here is to encourage everyone to participate in philanthropy. It's so easy to be involved that you don't even need to give away your money, you can donate mine!

Are you an Adventure Philanthropist too?

Since you've bought this book, I'm guessing you share some of my passion for travel, community service, and adventure. There's actually a lot of us out there, regular everyday people having an extraordinary impact with our lives.

Take my friend Jo from London. Jo runs a human resources division at a medium-sized corporation. Each year, Jo takes a month off to travel to a new region of the world. While there, she spends several weeks volunteering. I met Jo hiking to see the mountain gorillas in East Africa. When we parted, she was heading to Malawi to join a non-profit organization which encourages children to read and delivers books to remote areas of the country. Jo spent several weeks riding in a mobile library and reading to children.

Then there's Caroline and Nieve, best friends and British doctors who were working with the chronically ill in Sub-Saharan Africa. They'd finished their medical training and decided to do a gap year, travelling around Africa providing palliative care to those in need. When I met them in Kampala, the capital of Uganda, they were going into the city slums to administer pain medication to people suffering from HIV/AIDS and cancer.

Or check out my friends Peter and Helen, a former advertising executive and stylist respectively, and true New Yorkers. At the height of their careers, this married couple sold their Brooklyn loft and set out to explore the world. After several years of traveling, they settled in Bali to run a marine research center tracking the manta ray population in the warm Indonesian waters.

Each of these friends combined what they love to do with a charitable intent. And it's when they coupled their passions—encouraging children to read, attending the sick, or conducting environmental research—when their lives became extraordinary and they began living their dream.

The best part is you don't need to venture far and wide to be an Adventure Philanthropist. You can combine your passion and philanthropy right in your own back yard.

Like Tracy, who lives in Chicago, Illinois. Tracy's a mortgage broker with a passion for helping animals, particularly pit bulls who have been rescued from the fighting ring. To celebrate each mortgage she closes, she gives a donation to the local animal shelter to help care for injured and abandoned animals. Tracy is making a real difference in the lives of the abused animals she loves.

Or my friend Chris, a business manager with a massive software company. He's contacting local schools in San Francisco to provide technology audits. Once he assesses the school's hard and soft technology needs, he arranges for software donations and a technical team to come in to update the school's systems. He's found a way to combine his business skills with giving.

And how about Tom, the tow truck driver I met in Reno, Nevada. I met Tom when my car broke down and I needed a 3-hour tow to Sacramento. During the ride I learned that Tom, an outlaw biker, used to own a biker bar and hosted an annual poker run to raise money for one of his waitresses who had a child with a chronic disease. Eventually, the annual biker event was raising close to $10,000 each year to help the family with their medical bills.

Jo, Caroline & Nieve, Peter & Helen, Tracy, Chris, and Tom are just a few of the fabulous people I've met during my travels around the world. Everyday people who are combining their passions with philanthropy. They're making the world a better place and having a great time doing it.

They are all Adventure Philanthropists—and you can be one too!

Chapter 1: **HOPE**

I knew that at the end of my adventure, I would not be the same person who started my worldwide journey. I couldn't be. There was no way I could have all of these intense experiences and not be fundamentally changed. I would evolve. But the person I would evolve into was a mystery.

It was a beautiful late summer day in August 2010 and I was driving through California's majestic redwood forests. I had the sunroof open, I was singing at the top of my lungs, and I was thinking: "I could do this forever!"

It then occurred to me—I could do this forever.

I could embrace this feeling of exhilaration and exploration. I could keep hurtling myself forward. I could continue to race toward whatever lie beyond the next bend. And why stop at the U.S. border? Why not traverse the whole world?

In that moment it became clear to me that I was going to shelve my plans to buy a house, close up my consulting firm, and uproot myself from my family and friends. I would become a world nomad. I would travel the world for two years and explore to my heart's content.

I would volunteer, search out new cultures, and climb mountains, literally and figuratively.

In anticipation of total transformation, I steadfastly refused to commit to returning to America. In fact, I did everything I could to cut my strings to the States. The first to go were my material anchors. I gave up my apartment, sold my car and furniture, donated my clothes. All finances went online.

I then severed emotional ties. By not promising to return, I lost several friendships. I realize it's hard to be a friend, investing energy into a relationship, when you may never see that person again. While I mourned the loss of these friendships, I also understood that the uncertainty of my lifestyle made others uncomfortable. It's one thing to ask your friends to stay in touch. It's a much larger commitment to ask them to join you for a long-term emotional ride.

Finally, I shared the cherished artwork I had gathered from around the world with my friends and family. Tribal Moroccan rugs went to my friend Jane. A colorful hand-embroidered Mayan calendar was bestowed on the Cottrells. An intricate silver urn festooned with dragons and acquired in Mongolia was hand-delivered to my mother. I shut off my U.S. phone.

I was left with one file drawer of tax documents and a pile of personal mementos. During this final purge, I rigorously chose a couple of items that symbolized my closest relationships: letters from my father, a coat and cook book from my mother, videos of me and my brother as kids, personal talismans. All my earthly possessions now fit into two chest drawers. I was completely unencumbered.

What I was left with was my dream: to combine my passion for travel with my desire to give back.

I wanted to have experiences that forced an emotional response, created a consciousness, elicited dialogue, inspired me to learn and to grow. I wanted to learn and witness and participate in the larger world around me. This was my hope and the promise of my travels.

So while all around me people were wrapping their holiday gifts, I was wrapping up my life. With the New Year, I would start my new life, embracing the ultimate free fall as I leaped into the unknown. I had no safety net, but only the confidence that I could fly. And I had the whole world in which to spread my wings.

So I think my nomadic life was less about escaping a past or seeking a future, and more about embracing the present. Living life in the now. What follows is a tale of my two-year journey around the world. But it's not a chronological account of my trip, which began in Fiji on New Year's Eve 2010 and ended in Antarctica in 2012.

This is not a book about places, but a story about people. Fellow travelers who are fearless and fun and often foolhardy. Communities which are fighting to preserve their cultures and traditions. Children who are living, and sometimes thriving, despite unbelievable obstacles. Individuals I've met who are changing the world in ways I never dreamed of.

Auntie Claire – Culion, Philippines

It was mid-morning and I had just finished my breakfast of fruit and bread. I was on the Philippine island of Culion, which was once the world's largest leper colony. It was divided into *leproso* and *sano* (clean) sections. The clean side of the island is where non-afflicted healthcare workers and colony administrators lived.

Striking out before the sun and heat became relentless, I walked down a dirt road, heading toward the "leproso" cemetery. I was curious to know whether the unequal treatment of the leproso and sano populations endured even in death.

Hotel staff repeatedly advised me to take a rickshaw for my morning trek, warning me that the cemetery was too far to walk. But with a long afternoon free to explore, I decided to set out on foot anyway. Promptly getting lost, I was wandering about when Auntie Claire spotted me.

She was sitting in the doorway of a simple three-room house eating her lunch of rice and fish, sharing tidbits with her scrawny cat. Realizing I was adrift, she called me over and invited me into her home for tea. Auntie Claire suffered the horrible affliction that is more correctly known as Hansen's Disease. Leprosy had scarred her face and hands and feet, leaving her without most of her fingers, some of her toes and portions of her face.

Auntie Claire had spent sixty-five of her seventy years on Culion. Showing early signs of the disease, her parents had abandoned her at age five to the care of a Carmelite order of French nurse-nuns who ran the sanitarium. Auntie Claire lived in the girls' dormitory until she was sixteen years old, chafing under the nuns' strict rules. Her days were filled with praying and going to church and saying the rosary.

So Auntie Claire escaped, got married, and raised ten children: nine girls and a single boy. Though her husband left her for another woman thirty-eight years ago, she thinks it was a blessing since he was a drunkard and cruel to the children.

Auntie Claire now shares the house with one of her daughters, with her son living close by in the village. All of her other children have left, feeding the famous Filipino diaspora which sends millions of workers all over the world. Several of her girls are working in the Gulf; one an engineer, another an accountant.

Though she had been free of leprosy for many years, like many of the colony inmates (as they refer to themselves), Auntie Claire decided to stay on the island. After more than fifty years, the island prison had become her home.

Culion interested me because of its historic contribution to the field of medicine. I was curious about the inmates and their lives. I originally heard of the island from my friend Rick, a former Peace Corp volunteer in the Philippines.

I have never met Rick, but he is very active on my Facebook page. This is all I needed to heed his suggestion and plan my entire time in the Philippines around a visit to the island's budding eco-lodge run by Jesuit priests. Hotel Maya, where I stayed, is a training center for youth on the island, providing them job skills in the tourism industry.

I never figured out what the hotel's "eco" angle was exactly. Perhaps it was considered green since it only had electricity from 6:00 pm to 10:00 pm at night and no hot water. But it didn't matter. The young staff at the hotel were full of smiles. Of course, they had time to be friendly. I was the only tourist on the island. Leprosy tourism wasn't exactly thriving.

I ate alone at the hotel's restaurant each night. The hotel staff set my place at the table, not facing the open window and the scenic bay as I would have preferred, but directly across from a picture of *The Last Supper*. For three nights in a row, I ate my pre-ordered meal of a pork chop and rice in front of Jesus and the twelve Apostles. They were good companions.

I spent my days on the island quietly reading books about the history of the colony and visiting the local museum. I watched a very informative film and studied the pictures of the inmates, as well as the doctors and nurses who cared for them. I tried to absorb the details of their faces, to see what they were thinking and feeling as they lived out their lives in this island institution.

I became fascinated by the internal society that the inmates created, forming their own police force and musical band. Island inmates also served as teachers in the school and many of them became nurses and helped care for their fellow patients. And I learned all about the cure for Hansen's Disease.

I was actually relieved to find out that there was a cure. Per my normal approach to travel, I didn't do any research before I set off for my island destination. I merely showed up at the dock and hopped in the small wooden boat that Hotel Maya had arranged for me.

It was during the two-hour bumpy boat ride to Culion that I noticed my two escorts—a young lad from the hotel and the captain—were missing a few of their digits. This discovery gave me pause.

Only then did it dawn on me that I was going to a former leper colony. Uncharitable thoughts entered my head, like: "They have cured leprosy, haven't they? I mean, they wouldn't promote Culion as a tourist destination if the disease still exists, would they?"

I wish I'd thought of these questions the day before, when a quick online search would have provided some pertinent answers. But too late, I was left to wonder during the remainder of the boat ride, and silently, since I was too embarrassed to ask. It was a long ride.

To my great relief, I learned that the cure for Hansen's Disease was found in the mid-1980s. A treatment called Multiple Drug Therapy (MDT), created by researchers on the island and tested on Culion patients, was found to not only cure the onset of the disease, but actually retract the symptoms.

Patients took a regimen of pills each day and their lesions abated. If a patient was found to be lesion-free for two years, the patient was considered cured and allowed to leave the colony. In 1999, the World Health Organization declared leprosy eliminated on Culion, finding less than one in 10,000 cases existed.

It's amazing to me that a few pills swallowed each morning could eradicate this disfiguring disease that had tortured so many for so long. During my time at the colony, I became fascinated with the role that the Culion inmates and doctors played in finding a cure. I strived to put a face to the science and understand the sacrifices of the patients.

I learned a lot during my time on the island. I now know that leprosy isn't hereditary and not easily communicable. In fact, less than 10% of the world's population is even capable of catching the disease. Those who did contract leprosy most likely had a predisposition that was exacerbated by malnutrition and unsanitary conditions. These physical hardships were compounded by the emotional trauma of the disease. To be shunned, cast out by your community, is a horrific way to live.

I also learned that the leper colony of Culion was created during the American occupation of the Philippines in 1898. At the time, leprosy was ravaging the Philippine islands, with more than 25,000 people infected. The American solution was to set up a reservation modeled after the leper colony founded by Father Damien on the Hawaiian island of Molokai.

In 1906, the American colonial government formally opened the Culion Leper Colony and passed a *Segregation Law on Leprosy* which authorized the systematic collection and forced segregation of all persons afflicted with the disease.

Medical personnel and police would patrol the islands looking for the tell-tale signs of disfigurement. The afflicted, many of whom ran into the hills to escape capture, were hunted. Babies were taken from their mothers. Children separated from their families for life. Once apprehended, those already suffering were banished to the Culion prison—the penultimate purgatory.

The colony, first run by the Carmelite nuns, was later run by Jesuits priests. Both religious orders enforced strict governance. In fact, marriage was forbidden among the inhabitants. Well, forbidden until 142 babies were born one year. This out-of-wedlock coupling scandalized the nuns and priests and they finally gave in and legalized marriage in the colony, if only to save their patients' souls.

During the 20th century, the world still thought that leprosy was highly contagious and lepers had to be segregated from the rest of society. Not even parents and their children were spared. New parents on Culion were only able to keep their children for the first few months of their lives. Once the babies reached the six-month mark, they were removed to a hospital ward to be raised by nurses until it was determined whether or not the children carried the disease. During this enforced quarantine, parents could visit their children only once a week and view them through a glass pane. No touching allowed, lest the parents inadvertently infect their children.

At the age of six, the children were tested for signs of leprosy. If there were positive signs, the children were placed back at home with their parents. If not, the children were permanently relocated to an orphanage called Welfareville in Manila, never to see their family again. There was no joyous outcome for the parents. Either your child had inherited the disease or the child was taken away forever. A true tragedy.

This quarantine and forced removal of children is just one of many indignities that the Culion inmates suffered. The patients were also made to undergo experimental treatments, not all of which were successful. In the end, Culion patients played an instrumental role in finding a cure for their dreaded disease. It was their sacrifice of submitting themselves to rigorous research and testing that paved the way for a successful treatment and consequent cure for leprosy. This took incredible courage.

During my time on Culion, I discovered a clear message of hope. Cures for terrible diseases can be found. People can survive and even prosper despite deplorable conditions and inhumanity. A distained culture can reinvent itself as an island get-away of a better kind.

I consider my time spent in Culion a gift. I gained insight into a private world and took tea with a true survivor. Hearing Auntie Claire's life story was worth the trip itself. As I prepared to set off, she gave me a final piece of advice: "Take a rickshaw to the cemetery." And this time, I listened.

The Honorable Zenaye Tadesse – Ethiopia

Like lepers in the past, people suffering from HIV/AIDS in many parts of the world are shunned, making the virus not only a physically debilitating disease, but a social one.

As a region, Africa's suffering is acute. Although the continent only has 10% of the world's population, it has 68% of all new HIV/AIDS infections. In 2010, 1.5 million Africans became infected and 1.2 million Africans died of the disease. Perhaps most tragically, two-thirds of Africans living with the disease don't receive the medical treatment they need to survive.

Africa's women and children suffer the most: 75% of all women living with the malady reside in Africa and 9 out of 10 AIDS orphans are African. African women are especially vulnerable to HIV infection due to the region's widespread sexual violence both inside and outside of marriage. Sexual violence damages the reproductive tissues and increases the risk of HIV transmission to women.

Further exacerbating the problem, African women must cope with harmful traditional practices such as early marriage, genital mutilation, and wife inheritance. This entrenched societal inequality makes it difficult for the region's women to negotiate condom use and the safe sex practices that could keep them free of infection.

Rather than being overwhelmed by the scale of the problem, Africans are finding ways to combat the pandemic, both in terms of medical treatment and societal acceptance. In 2010, The **National Network of Positive Women Ethiopia (NNPWE)** hosted its first beauty pageant for HIV+ women.

While I'm not usually a fan of beauty contests, this one is special. There were twenty contestants, each representing their hometown. To encourage participation, they each received 1,000 Birr for entering (about $56), more than a two-week wage in Ethiopia.

The judges evaluated the contestants on a number of attributes, including stage control, smile, confidence, audience connection, and general knowledge about HIV/AIDS. Ethiopia is known for its beautiful women and competition was fierce, with regional rivalries kicking in.

The winner and first Ms. HIV+ Ethiopia was Bethlehem Gebre, representing the region of Hawassa located in the Great Rift Valley. In addition to the pageant crown and title, Bethlehem received 5,000 Birr (nearly $280), the equivalent of three months' salary in Ethiopia.

While the judges were evaluating the contestant's physical beauty, there is a deeper beauty within this competition because these women publicly announced their HIV+ status. Wide coverage in national and local media helped NNPWE reach one of its main objectives: to present accomplished, beautiful Ethiopian women who are HIV+, thereby challenging the stigma surrounding the disease.

It was hoped that this public appreciation and applause for women who are HIV+ would help break down the discrimination that keeps many women from seeking treatment. The Ms. HIV+ Ethiopia pageant is a small but significant step toward reducing some of the ugliness that festers within the African AIDS epidemic.

While I was in the capital Addis Ababa I gave a fundraising seminar to more than forty grassroots organizations working to combat HIV/AIDS. The seminar, on fundraising tactics and the overseas donor market, was organized by my friend Gashaw and hosted by the AIDS Resource Center, a quasi-governmental organization.

In addition to the seminar, I chose two organizations to work with in more depth, helping the management teams formulate business development plans. One was NNPWE, the other organization was the *Ethiopian Women's Lawyers Association (EWLA),* dedicated to strengthening women's rights in the country.

I developed a fast friendship with the head of the organization, Zenaye Tadesse. Formerly a federal judge, Zenaye and her team of lawyers were desperate to find funding. In 2011, the Ethiopian government passed a law mandating that the majority of funding intended for nonprofit organizations needed to come from local sources. This law is most stringently applied to Ethiopian-based organizations protecting human rights.

This new law means that EWLA can't accept foreign funding, the source of almost all of their income to date, without also securing significant local funds. We worked hard, spending several days brainstorming ways to raise money locally—quite a challenge in one of the most cash-strapped countries in the world. I'm happy to say that by the end we had developed a viable fundraising plan.

Over the week we worked together, we also went to breakfast and lunch and shopped together, as most women like to do. One of the benefits of volunteering while traveling is meeting the locals and forming friendships, seeing the issues first-hand that are affecting the country, and checking out the neighborhood joints. This is the way to really get to know a country.

In Ethiopia, this meant participating in elaborate coffee-serving ceremonies and being treated to arguably the best coffee in the world. It also means shared a traditional *injera* lunch. Injera, a large, hub-cap sized pancake of fermented *teff,* a type of grain, is the basis of every Ethiopian meal. With your right hand, you pull off a piece of the sponge-like injera, and dip it into the spicy side dishes.

On my last day in the city, Zenaye took me shopping for a *shema,* a traditional Ethiopian white shawl. According to tradition, women and men must wear white when entering an Ethiopian Orthodox church, and since most Ethiopians attend mass once, if not several times a day, you see the iconic white shema everywhere.

At the local textile market, we found the best quality shema made with finely woven linen and beautiful hand-embroidered edges. I was going to buy two, one for me and one as a gift for my mother. To my great surprise and delight, Zenaye bought me a shema as a thank you gift for my volunteer work. Touched by this kind gesture, I chose the scarf with the lavender flower border because violet is Zenaye's favorite color and it would remind me of her.

During our shopping excursion, I was also looking for a traditional long-flowing Ethiopian dress. I had seen women wearing them while shoulder-dancing in local bars and I wanted one too. Shoulder dancing is a traditional Ethiopian form of entertainment, where the women stand in front of you and shrug their shoulders up and down in time to the music. It's strangely seductive.

Since I so admired the culture, I thought an ethnic Ethiopian party dress would be the perfect souvenir. I decided to splurge, making room in my suitcase by swapping out an item of clothing. A pair of dull khaki hiking pants were enthusiastically exchanged for a billowy white dress with elaborate green and gold embroidery on the waist and trim. Fancy!

Shopping complete, we headed to a local bar to celebrate our purchases and drink 20-cent bottles of beer. During this festive happy hour, I almost gave into dares to change into my new party dress and model it for the bar patrons. Luckily, I didn't. When I got it home and tried it on, I found out that the white fabric was completely transparent. Disaster averted, but it was a close one.

Later that night, I said my farewells to my friends. I needed to be up the next morning at 4:00 am to catch my flight to South Africa. During the eight-hour flight to the opposite end of the continent, I had plenty of time to think about my new-found friends and their lives. I reflected on the ravages of disease, the depths of discrimination, the paradoxical demonstrations of faith.

I also thought about the country's slim, yet powerful, signs of hope: the Ms. HIV+ Ethiopia contestants bravely walking the pageant runway and Zenaye, a judge who chooses to use her skills to help bolster women's rights. These are women to watch. These are women of hope.

Dr. Simon Pierce – Tofo, Mozambique

Once on Southern African soil, I was fortunate to meet a man who inspired hope. Dr. Simon Pierce, or Dr. Simon as I call him, is dedicating his life to saving a single species: whale sharks. Based in the small beach town of Tofo in southern Mozambique, he runs a research center called the *Marine Megafauna Foundation* which seeks to identify and solve the problems that whale sharks face throughout the world: namely, possible annihilation.

See, we humans are killing our megafauna, the term used for large marine life such as sharks, rays, marine mammals, and turtles. Not only do megafauna live a long time, on average seventy years, but they also have low reproductive rates. Consequently, their populations are usually the first to be squeezed by human pressures and many are in danger of extinction.

I met Dr. Simon while attending a lecture he gave on whale sharks in the backroom of a bar. During this very informative presentation, I learned that whale sharks are the world's largest fish. They can grow to more than 40 feet (12 m) in length and weigh more than 45,000 lbs (20 kg).

Whale sharks are also the deepest diving fish, capable of plunging nearly a mile (two km) to the bottom of the ocean. As a species they originated more than sixty million years ago. Yet despite knowing a thing or two about survival, their future is under threat.

Dr. Simon told us how the Marine Megafauna Foundation goes about its work, researching and protecting the large populations of marine megafauna found along the Mozambican coastline, including 18% of the world's known whale shark population.

After the presentation, I introduced myself to Dr. Simon as a professional fundraiser and potential volunteer. I happened to be staying at the lodge where the research center was based, so we made a quick plan for me to drop by the research center the next afternoon.

We met several times that week to discuss fundraising strategies. One of the benefits of volunteering at the research center was that I got to hang out with other research center volunteers: Peter, Helen, Katie and Daan. This was a fun group of people! And it happened to be Katie's 24th birthday, which made that week a full-on good time.

I had stumbled upon the folks of Marine Megafauna by sheer chance. I was in staying in Tofo, about a ten-hour mini-bus ride north of Mozambique's capital Maputo. I had envisioned hanging out at the beach for a few days, then heading further north to the beach scene at Vilanculos. But I liked Tofo and got a little stuck.

It was my birthday that week too, albeit I was turning forty-four, rather than twenty-four, years of age. Each year as a birthday present to myself I learn something new. It's a way for me to push my own boundaries and try things I find intimidating. In previous years, I went sky diving and got my scuba diving certification. I took West African dance classes and learned to ride a horse. This year, I wanted to learn how to surf.

While I grew up in California and Hawaii and knew plenty of surfers, I still didn't know how to surf. So the morning of my birthday, I hired a surf instructor named Clayton. As Clayton was giving me some basic instructions, he spotted a juvenile humpback whale breeching in the waters right off shore. There we stood, Clayton and I with a surfboard between us, watching this incredible whale leap again and again into the air. What a great birthday gift!

I turned out to be mediocre surfer, although I had a fabulous time. I got my first taste of how much fun surfing could be—especially if you manage to stand up. Weirdly, I got worse as the morning progressed and after a few hours, I returned Clayton's rash guard and headed back to my beach hut.

My birthday abode was a reed hut with a sand floor and palm leaves covering a tin roof. Mosquito netting kept the mozzies out at night, but this didn't help with the fleas that were in the bedding. That morning I woke up with seventeen flea bites on the left side of my face. It was not an attractive look.

Since it was my birthday week, I felt that I deserved clear skin so I took myself off to grander digs down the beach, where I found the folks at Marine Megafauna. While I was there, I swam with the whale sharks three times. With each occasion, I was a little less terrified.

As filter fish, whale sharks mostly eat plankton. Their mouths open nearly 5 feet (1.5 m) wide and contain 300 rows of tiny teeth. The first time you see this wide toothy grin it's a bit disconcerting. Especially when the enormous whale shark is swimming directly toward you. Rationally you know they don't eat people, and yet, sometimes a mistake is made. I took this opportunity to test a long-held theory. It's true—no one can hear you scream underwater.

My first sighting of this fire engine-sized fish coming toward me sent me swimming back to the boat. But the next time, after an initial sprint in the opposite direction, I managed to re-gain my composure and circle back to the whale shark, tailing him from behind. It was a very cool experience to be swimming in the ocean with one of its largest creatures.

I liked the experience so much that I decided to adopt a whale shark of my own. That month for my **Donate My Dollars** poll, I chose to sponsor a whale shark and let my web site readers pick a name. The winner was *Kubwa Ya Moyo* which means "Big Heart" in Swahili.

Kubwa Ya Moyo is an 18 foot (6 m) female whale shark. To identify her, researchers take a picture underwater using two laser beams projected onto her skin, just behind the gills. The laser points provide a set marker in which to measure the immense size of the fish.

Another way to identify her is through a unique pattern of dots that is found on each whale shark. This freckling is as individual as a finger print. Kubwa Ya Moyo, with her own unique set of freckles, is registered as MZ-620 in the Global Whale Shark Database, a worldwide photo-identification library that catalogues each known whale shark.

Each time a whale shark is sighted, an identification is made via the catalogue with the time, place, and depth of the sighting recorded. The library is maintained and used by marine biologists around the world, providing insight into whale shark habitats, behaviors, and migration patterns.

As a foster parent, I'm notified whenever Kubwa Ya Moyo is sighted. I hope that one day I'll run into her while scuba diving in Thailand's Similan Islands. Or in the Indian Ocean off Sri Lanka. Or perhaps in Sipadan in the mighty Pacific. There are an estimated 3,500 whale sharks in existence, so this is a small hope.

My larger hope is that the Marine Megafauna Foundation will be able to continue to make great strides in the global conservation of this threatened species. Just as I hope that the stigma of HIV/AIDS in Africa will diminish and the millions of people living with the disease will receive the medical treatment that can save their lives.

I hope that medical researchers will find a cure for AIDS, just as they found a cure for leprosy. I hope that those who suffer from the disease, particularly women, can be released from their prisons of isolation and society's bigotry. These are my big hopes.

Chapter 2: **HUMILITY**

As I sat on the local mini bus (starting) out the window, I saw what looked like a scene straight out of the Middle Ages. There were open sewers, livestock roaming the streets, starving children in tatters. I gasped.

I was in Gonder, Ethiopia and it was here that I saw a man so poor he didn't have any clothes to wear. Not a religious person, I nevertheless sent up a prayer. Not for those mired in poverty, but out of concern for myself. "Please God, do not let this be my bus stop."

Coming face-to-face with the stark reality of extreme poverty for the first time, I was humbled. And incredulous. How could a place like this exist in our modern world? I was also ashamed that my first thought was for myself.

About 318 million people live in extreme poverty, which is defined as living on less than $1.25 a day. In 1998, the World Bank classified 61 countries as low–income or "poor." By 2001, the number of extremely poor nations had decreased to 39 countries. This is a great improvement, with countries such as India, Indonesia, Nigeria, and Pakistan moving out of extreme poverty to middle-income status.

2013 1.2 billion in extreme poverty
World bank wants to end extreme poverty by 2030

But while most countries in East Asia and South Asia are making steady gains, the poverty rate in Africa is increasing, both in terms of absolute numbers, due to higher birth rates, and as a higher percentage of people living in extreme poverty. So in Africa, there are a greater number of people living in poverty and they are getting poorer. A double whammy.

During my trip I saw a great deal of poverty close up. Close enough to sense dejection. Close enough to see thirst. Close enough to taste sorrow.

Lois – Zambia-Malawi Border

It took me three days, two coach buses, one minivan, two shared taxis, and three regular taxis to complete the trip from Livingstone, Zambia, to Lilongwe, the capital of Malawi, a country where 90% of its population live on under $2 a day. It was here that I got to meet a woman named Lois, who represented foreign charities in Malawi. Lois showed me the human side of poverty. She also served me my first slice of Humble Pie.

Lois told me about the struggles of women in rural Malawi who need to travel great distances to receive medical care during pregnancy and delivery. This burden is due to a misguided government policy stipulating that pregnant women should deliver their children in medical clinics, instead of in their home villages with the assistance of a local midwife, as has been done for centuries. And so when women enter labor or nearly, they are escorted by the midwife to the nearest medical clinic, sometimes enduring a multi-day journey.

The journey to the medical centers is a physically tough one. Since there are almost no private cars in rural areas, a laboring woman is usually transported by bike. Often the impending mother sits on the bike, while the midwife pushes from behind. Lois explained that, despite this arduous journey, when the woman finally makes it to the health clinic, she is frequently denied medical care. Why? There are no rubber gloves.

And without adequate protection, doctors and nurses in this part of sub-Saharan Africa do not risk HIV/AIDS infection. So in the end, after a grueling, uncomfortable, and painful multi-day journey, the rural midwife is still the one to deliver the child. Truly unimaginable.

A series of questions ricocheted through my head upon hearing this story: "How much can a box of rubber gloves cost? Couldn't we just buy cases to distribute to medical centers? Why would the government ask these women to travel long distance to receive medical care that was then declined once they arrived?" My frustration was mounting.

Not only was the journey physically perilous for these pregnant women, but also emotionally draining. One of the women's main concerns was that if they had to travel overnight they would need to take a blanket. It was Lois who explained to me the importance of blankets for a family. Since the children sleep with their parents in one bed, they all share one blanket. So if the mother-to-be took the blanket with her to the medical clinic, her husband and children would have nothing to keep them warm as they slept.

Lois' explanation gave me great pause. I'd noticed during my three-day bus ride that the locals were often carrying blankets in clear plastic duvet covers. I assumed that each traveler had wrapped the blanket around something precious that they were carrying on their trip. It never occurred to me that it was the blanket itself that was valuable. I found it unimaginable that a blanket was the family's most prized possession.

This realization about the importance of what I considered an everyday item is one of the most humbling moments during my trek and one that will stick. To me, a blanket is no longer just a blanket. It will always symbolize the warmth of a family, the closeness of children as they sleep, an irreplaceable comfort during childbirth. A family in Malawi is lucky to have a blanket. And I am lucky to have learned the value of a blanket.

Even within extreme levels of poverty in Africa, I noticed subtle dividing lines. Someone who doesn't even own a pair of shoes indicates a deeper level of poverty. Engraved in my memory is the image of a young man wearing one broken plastic shoe. In his world, one shoe was better than no shoe, even if that one was plastic with holes in it. It still had a sole. And I suppose on some level, that one shoe emboldened his soul.

Clothing is another obvious indication of poverty. In many African countries, it's not uncommon to see young children, especially those under the age of five, not wearing pants. (I figured this was for potty-training reasons in a world without diapers.) But when older children, and especially adults, have no clothes, it is a tragic indicator. My first experience with a man in tatters was years ago in a village in Tanzania. A friend and I were walking together on a dirt path bordering a national park. The man stepped out in front of us, facing us square on. He was challenging us, insisting that we see him. What I saw was sheer desperation in his eyes.

Houses likewise tell a story. Like the *Three Little Pigs* fable, houses in Africa are built of straw, sticks, or bricks. In Namibia, we passed by entire villages made of straw huts, each house partially hidden in the folds of the sandy dunes. And the countryside in Zambia is dotted with stick houses that couldn't withstand a gust of wind.

The use of roofing materials in particular can be indicative of a family's relative wealth. Palm leaves for roofs are seen throughout semi-tropical Mozambique. Tin roofs are a step above, and tile roofs are considered a luxury item. Windows are also a status symbol—whether there is a plastic covering, a wooden shutter, or in the most elaborate homes, glass window panes.

What I found most heartening to observe during my overland journeys is the care taken with many of these homes. Even when a house has a palm roof and no window coverings, the court yard will be swept clean of debris. Oftentimes you'll spy flowering trees and plants surrounding the doorway. Or a touch of paint added to a wooden window sill.

These types of adornments indicate a pride of home ownership that is uplifting to see. We all must deal with the circumstances we've been dealt, and yet to see care taken in one's home, even in areas suffering from entrenched poverty, is inspiring. These house-proud dwellings symbolize the resilience of the families that live there.

As I stared out the bus window, these were my musings on the importance and meaning of shelter. And so I spent the long hours in transit chewing on another healthy serving of humble pie.

Ker & Mae Nam - Namno Mountains, Laos

While I most often traveled overland by bus, I also sampled other forms of transport, like riding elephants. My elephant's name was Mae Nam. She was fifty-one years old and had a two-year-old infant. Mae Nam is known as the boss of the herd. As the matriarch, she displayed characteristics that are more generally associated with male elephants: aggression, dominance, orneriness.

I was visiting *Elephant Village*, an elephant sanctuary several hours outside of Luang Prabang, Laos' delightful second city. The sanctuary was on the banks of the Khan River, in the shadow of the Namno Mountain range and surrounded by lush jungle.

In the early 1800s, the camp was a training site for elephants participating in the royal procession. Known then as the "Land of a Million Elephants," Laos revered its national icon. Sadly today the number of wild elephants in Laos has fallen to less than 2,000.

Elephant Village's mission is to give rescued elephants a new home where they are free from heavy work, such as hauling logs through the forest. Instead, they earn their keep by giving rides to tourists. no! Our tourist dollars help pay for the elephant's food and care—which is substantial. Each day an elephant consumes at least 550 lbs. (250 kg) of grasses, bark, leaves, and fruit.

Elephant Village also offers local villagers an alternative to a slash-and-burn subsistence that prevails in the surrounding jungle. Each elephant has its own *mahout*, or trainer, who stays with the elephant their entire lives. Mae Nam's mahout is Ker. He'd been with her for the last eight years and accepts her idiosyncrasies.

Each of us became acquainted with our elephants by riding them around camp. Riding an elephant is trickier that it would appear. First, an elephant is pretty tough to get on. I tried several times, but in the end I had to be pushed by my butt to get up high enough to swing my leg over. Sometimes your elephant will cooperate by lying down or bending on one knee. If this happens, you step on her lower leg and pull yourself up by her ear.

WTF.

To control the elephant, the mahouts carry a mean-looking metal hook, like a giant knitting needle, that they jab behind the elephant's ear. The sharp pain stops the elephant from running away. I found it distressing to watch when Ker resorted to the hook with Mae Nam.

We spent the day helping care for our new charges. By late afternoon a group of ten of us rode our elephants across the river and into the jungle to tuck the elephants in for the night at a safe distance from the village. Intelligent as they are, an elephant can do a lot of damage and even demolish a village if they go on a rampage.

The next morning, with dawn breaking through the dense trees, we set off on the long hike back into the jungle to retrieve our trunked charges. Riding the elephants back, we crossed a river, stopping to give them their morning bath. Elephants clearly love water, submerging themselves and swishing their tails as we used stiff brushes to scrub the top of their heads and behind their ears. They had gotten surprisingly filthy after a night spent in their jungle clearing.

Mae Nam was especially fond of the bathing ritual and liked to totally submerge herself in the water, with me and Ker standing high on her back trying in vain to keep from falling in. Elephants will wallow in the water for as long as you let them, so we let her soak and splash for more than an hour.

During my short elephant-sitting session, I not only formed a bond with Mae Nam, but also a healthy respect for her size, intelligence, and individual personality. If she flapped her ears and swayed her trunk and tail, these were signs that Mae Nam was relaxed. However, if she suddenly stopped and stood still, staring intently, or put her trunk in her mouth, it was time to hand the reins over to the trained mahout.

The time spent learning about elephants first-hand was great fun and I was pleased that the fee for my tour not only helped support elephant rehabilitation, but also provided new economic and job opportunities to a rural village. Adventure Philanthropy at its best!

To top off the experience, the sanctuary surroundings were gorgeous and I enjoyed a plush room, (by my standards anyway), complete with a bed and mosquito net, balcony overlooking the river, and bathroom outfitted with indoor plumbing. Swank!

After full days of elephant excitement, we guests dined on an open-air veranda overlooking the lazy gray-brown river. Deep in the heart of the Laotian jungle, the riverside lodge had a very *Out of Africa* colonial atmosphere. Adding to this traditional feel, my fellow guests and I would meet up each evening, lingering at the communal dinner tables, and swap travel stories as the sun set.

One night, as we were settling deep into our chairs after dinner, our guide asked if he could borrow the headlamps we seasoned travelers relied on to get about after dark. The kitchen crew wanted to go bullfrog hunting and the lamps were the perfect instrument, allowing them to stun the frogs with the bright light while one's hands were free to scoop up the jumping amphibians. We gladly forked them over.

A little less than an hour later, our kitchen crew returned with their apron pockets stuffed with big, meaty bullfrogs. We heard them, animated and laughing in the kitchen, immensely enjoying their own dinner party and froggy feast.

It's possible that our Laotian buddies had picked up the taste for frog's legs during French colonial times. Although I believe a more plausible explanation is that the locals learned to eat the amphibian protein during the hard years, when the U.S. military was fighting its secret war in the Laotian countryside during the 1960s and early 1970s.

The frog feast triggered recollections of stories I had heard of my own family's readiness to eat alternative forms of food in lean times. For instance, during the Depression my mother's family, not long arrived from their homeland of Slovakia, took to raising frogs in their suburban Akron basement. The croaking creatures offered the family a real source of sustenance during those hungry years.

On our last evening at the elephant camp, a power outage forced us to reluctantly abandon the revelry of the dining room. A common-enough occurrence in the middle of the thick Southeast Asian jungle, we all returned to our rooms early and went to bed.

Before tucking myself into the mosquito netting, I put on my headlamp and made a trip to the bathroom at the end of the dark hall. When I returned, I snuggled down and read by the light of my headlamp, drifting off to sleep. Sometime in the middle of the night the power snapped back on. Groggily I made my way to hit the light switch and then stumbled back to bed. In my half-sleep state, it didn't dawn on me to check whether or not the bathroom light had also flickered on.

It had and unfortunately I'd left the door slightly ajar. Room enough for a passing termite.

Next morning, barely awake and rubbing my eyes, I was dumbstruck when I returned to the water closet. Drawn by the bright light, the winged ones had swarmed the small commode, covering the tile and fixtures several inches deep. The critters crunched underfoot as I took to the toilet, carefully hovering over the insect-encrusted seat. A shower was out of the question and I even vacated the inundated space to brush my teeth, opting instead to use bottled water and spit toothpaste foam from the relative safety of my veranda.

Packing to leave later that morning, I had no idea how to clean up the massive pile of insects. I was appalled at the mess I'd caused for the cleaning crew and assumed that someone would have to hose down the restroom, sweeping the soggy critters down the drain. But I was wrong.

On my way to breakfast, I passed two Lao ladies rushing towards my bathroom. They were carrying trays full of winged termites, salvaged from another lighted latrine. They then went to work on my overrun washroom, meticulously lifting each termite by the wings and placing them on their trays.

"They were painstakingly picking through the carnage to find the ones that were still alive," I said to a German traveler over breakfast. "I can't imagine why."

She explained to me that what I considered a terribly messy mishap was a boon for our Laotian hosts. You see, winged termites are a local delicacy and I had unwittingly provided an opportunity for them to collect hundreds. The barely alive insects were soon headed to the grill to be roasted over an open flame.

Like frogs, insects are seen as a rich source of food to the impoverished people of Laos. Laotians have been suffering chronic food shortages for more than fifty years. The harsh conditions that began with the secret American war and perpetual bombing, continued under the rule of their own communist government. Adding to the misery was an international embargo that denied the starving country international aid for decades.

Enduring decades of economic isolation, Laos is still dealing with crushing poverty. And, as so often happens, the normal folk are the ones paying the highest price. Faced with starvation, Laotians have adapted their diet to include sources of food that they would never have eaten in the past. Bugs and frogs are no longer jungle pests, but jungle prizes that can fill a bloated belly and provide needed nutrition.

Seeing the altered eating habits caused by decades of hunger was sobering. Just thinking back on the excitement of our kitchen crew elated with the capture of their froggy feast and the clean-up crew preparing for a winged BBQ was grim for me. I gained valuable insight on how people in other parts of the world perceive food and a new perspective on one of our most basic human needs—feeding one's self and family.

When a population is reduced to eating insects to stay alive, in my mind, you've crossed over to another level of poverty. My initial disgust with the winged termite infestation led me to a personal discovery and deeper understanding about the extent and power of hunger. And another hearty serving of humble pie.

William, Kate & the Kitten - Laos

After my elephant escapades, I returned to Luang Prabang to soak up its unspoiled Buddhist culture. Every day robed monks called a cheerful *"Sa-bai-dee,"* "How are you doing," as they pedaled past on the empty streets. Two of my favorite ways to observe Buddhist rituals are sitting outside the temples listening to the monks chanting at sunset and getting up before dawn to observe the monks' alms procession called *Tak Bat.*

Tak Bat takes place every morning at 6:00 am and lasts about fifteen minutes. The tradition of providing food for the monks is a way for the faithful to show humility, which Buddhists believe is the first step on the path towards nirvana.

Arriving just before sunrise, the city's devout Buddhists kneel quietly on the sidewalk, raise their rice basket to their forehead to bless the rice and issue a prayer. The townspeople then wait patiently for the saffron-robed monks to appear.

Slowly streaming out of the city temples, the monks silently walk down Sisavangvong Road, Luang Prabang's main street, with a rice bowl at their hip. As the monks silently pass, each believer places a small handful of sticky rice into the low-slung bowl. During the entire ceremony neither the laypeople distributing the rice nor the monks say a word. The procession of the silent monks in the early morning hours coupled with the quiet sincerity of the laypeople as they present their offerings, make this an incredibly poignant form of religious expression.

There's a strict etiquette to the Tak Bat ceremony. For instance, participants should either be sitting or kneeling so that they are lower than the monks passing by and worshippers must never touch the monks while handing out the food.

There's also a code of conduct for observers. It's important to be dressed modestly and stay quiet (no talking, no cell phones, no car horns). Equally disruptive are flash cameras that disrupt the sanctity of the ceremony. I decided to watch the procession from the opposite side of the street, sitting silently on a stoop, with a large shawl wrapped around me. I took very few pictures, opting instead to immerse myself in the beauty that was paraded before me.

While I made a conscious decision not to participate in the alms-giving ceremony, some tourists do. Purchasing rice, usually of inferior quality (which is an insult to the monks), from street vendors, foreign visitors take their place on the sidewalk to hand out rice to the passing monks. In my mind, I equate the alms-giving procession with the act of taking communion in the Christian Church. If you're not baptized, it would be presumptuous, and offensive to believers, to participate in this sacred ceremony.

The Tak Bat ceremony is indeed magical and one of the many traditions that makes life in Laos extraordinary. Another daily ritual is the nightly chanting at the temple, where monks gather at the end of the day to meditate.

Starting about 5:30 pm, monks and novices file into their temples, sit on the floor facing away from the door, and chant for almost an hour. I would plan my day so I could visit different temples to observe this nightly tradition. Perching myself unobtrusively in the shadows outside on the temple steps, I would sit quietly, draped in a large shawl, and listen to the sonorous serenade.

It was here on the temple steps that I met my first temple cat. A small black kitten, it reminded me of the kitties I had fostered from an animal shelter back at home. I felt an immediate attachment and visited my new friend almost every day, bringing the malnourished kitten a bit of milk and a small saucer to drink from. Placing my worry of flea bites aside, I would sit and cuddle the kitty as the monks inside the temple chanted in a hypnotic monotone. Looking back, those stints squatting at my temple observation post were some of my truest moments of peace and relaxation during my entire journey.

Late one afternoon, on my way to the temple, I stopped at a corner store to buy a pint-sized serving of milk for my furry friend. The proprietress was very excited to see me and kept gesturing to the TV she had on at the back of the store. On the screen was the wedding of Prince William and his bride Kate. The merchant was watching the wedding ceremony, enraptured with the regal proceedings. I, in turn, was delighted that she was so moved by the spectacle.

She kept giggling about the nuptials, pulling my arm for me to come and watch with her. I tried to explain to her that I was American and therefore slightly removed from the emotion of the English pomp and circumstance. But to her, we foreigners were all one, and she was thrilled to be able to share this bit of history with someone from that faraway place.

In the end, I just smiled and stood beside her, sharing a bit of camaraderie over the splendidly bedecked British royals. Our standing there watching together made me appreciate how small the world really is. Humble pie serving #3.

Reaksmey – Battambang, Cambodia

Neighboring Laos is the mystical Kingdom of Cambodia. While staying in Phnom Penh, I was introduced to a woman named Miriam, an American expat who had relocated to Cambodia's capital to work as a teacher. Miriam was also a woman with a cause and her cause was saving Sombo, a much loved resident of Phnom Penh. Sombo is a temple elephant, beloved by the locals, and a veritable institution in this city.

Sombo lived in two temples, one during the day and one at night. This joint custody arrangement meant that Sombo had to travel down the city's most heavily trafficked artery twice a day, schlepping on the scorching pavement, dodging motorbikes.

Miriam's goal was to raise money for a new nightly shelter at the daytime temple which would eliminate the need for Sombo to take his evening stroll down Main Street. During dinner one night, we discussed Miriam's options for raising money. I kept suggesting that Sombo give up his urban lifestyle and retire to the countryside, to live out his days in peace at an elephant sanctuary like the one I had just visited in northern Laos.

But Miriam wouldn't hear of it and neither would the population of Phnom Penh that loved him so. To me, this was an interesting lesson in fundraising. As a donor, you need to remember that you're helping people raise money for what they want, not necessarily for what you want. In this case what I wanted was a little rest and relaxation for this hard-working animal. But this wasn't an option. Sombo was too well-loved to be let go.

So I deferred to my host and strident public opinion on the matter of Sombo, offering several fundraising strategies that Miriam could deploy among her expat friends. But in truth, my heart wasn't really into it. I was cringing instead at the memory of Sombo weaving in and out of the cars during the city's raging rush hour.

Miriam and I had our fundraising conversation at a restaurant overlooking the Tonle Sap River, enjoying a performance by Cambodia's famous Aspara dancers. During our meal, Miriam told me about her friend Reaksmey, who was based in the Cambodian city of Battambang and working for a nonprofit called ***Phare Ponleu Selpak***. Translated as "the brightness of art," Phare Ponleu Selpak (PPS) harnesses the healing power of art and theater to help children cope with traumatic experiences. PPS is best known for its traveling circus. Now this is a mission I could get behind!

So I decided to travel to Battambang. Nabbing a one-way ticket on a local delivery boat, I set sail on the Tonlé Sap River. Crammed to capacity, I grabbed my life vest (Ha ha! there are no life vests!) and promptly alighted to the boat's roof, where I remained for most of the trip. By this point I was a seasoned Southeast Asia wooden boat traveler and knew the safest place was up top, which offered the small possibility to jump clear if the boat started to sink.

By mid-day, the sun was scorching, so I used my umbrella for a bit of shade. I listened to music and watched the floating river villages of Cambodia drift past. It was fascinating to get a glimpse of life on the Tonlé Sap River, with schools, houses, and shops all bobbing in our wake. Besides hauling cargo and passengers, the boat also served as the local mail delivery system and people would eagerly paddle out to our boat in an assortment of small craft to collect packages and mail letters.

The children living in the floating villages were excited to see the boat slide by, yelling out greetings and waving. Yet as we made our way inland, the villages on the banks grew noticeably poorer. After a few hours, I began to see the effects of dire poverty etched on people's faces. The children were still playful, but the adults in this part of the country stared with angry eyes. The people living here were too thin and unkempt and not particularly keen to have us passengers observe their plight.

Finally in late afternoon, at the threat of rain, I climbed down inside the boat and rejoined my fellow travelers. For the next two hours, a tropical storm pelted the small boat, with droplets leaking in from the roof and river water seeping in from hull. I squeezed into a seat next to a young man, who was missing most of his hands. At the time, I didn't think about it, but in retrospect I believe he was suffering from leprosy.

The young man and I exchanged pleasantries, mostly through friendly gestures, head nods, and smiles. He showed me a turtle peeking out of his bag. At first I thought it was an enormous snake and almost peed my pants, but then I noticed the shell. When he uncovered his precious cargo, the foreign tourists behind us kept cooing at his pet. But I knew better. That large turtle wasn't a pet he was transporting to his family, but dinner to be feasted upon later that night. The turtle, suffering in his cardboard box, had only hours left to live.

After more than ten hours on this advertised seven-hour trip, we arrived. In the waning light, I flagged a driver who helped load my luggage. Balancing my huge suitcase on his head, he skillfully walked the narrow wooden plank leading to shore. Before I knew it, he had whisked me away into his tuk tuk and we were speedily splashing through puddles along the muddy road.

I arrived at the guest house wet and tired and famished. (The bread and cheese I had bought for the day trip had turned out to be moldy.)

After a quick shower, I headed right to the hotel restaurant. As the waiter and I bantered, I told him I was there to see the circus. He informed me that the circus only performs one night a week and tonight was my lucky night. I scarfed my meal, bought a ticket, and arranged a ride to and from the event. I was going to the circus!

But this was no ordinary circus. The PPS spectacle was created in a refugee camp on the Thai-Cambodian border. With an original cast of eight students, the volunteer art teacher decided to create a local theater production to help the young refugees deal with their grisly upbringing in the rough refugee center.

But I didn't really know all this back-story when I eagerly took my seat in the bleachers. I was here to see a circus and anticipated the usual antics. What I saw was anything but conventional.

A series of theatrical acts were performed, each portraying increasingly unsavory experiences. There were actors pantomiming *pedophilia episodes. Clowns with exaggerated expressions, leering at the children. Jugglers tossing what appeared to be bombs.* This slapstick was anything but silly. It was scary.

But the audience around me was howling with laughter. Filled with locals, more than half of the attendees were children, who are allowed to come to the circus for free. With the whole performance conducted in the Lao language, I tried to convince myself that I didn't understand what was occurring under the Big Top. But I did.

The circus was formed as a way to provide art therapy to troubled youth. The performance I was watching was a form of psychotherapy that encouraged creativity and self-expression as a way for children to deal with traumatic experiences. I was eating popcorn and witnessing a young girl's assault at the hands of a lecherous uncle. It was all I could do not to gag.

As the performance progressed, it tackled the all-too-real experiences of these young Cambodian children. The jugglers were indeed parodying the proliferation of unexploded land mines throughout the country. And the clowning around addressed issues of drug addiction, the prevalence of child prostitution, and the reality of cross-border human trafficking.

The young actors, often with first-hand experience of the scenes they performed, are helping to warn others of the dangers that prey upon vulnerable youth. By performing throughout the Cambodian countryside at schools, hospitals, and markets, the circus performers are helping create awareness and dialogue about the harsh reality for far too many Cambodian kids.

After I got home that night, I tried to digest all I had seen that day. I lay awake wondering what could have brought a society to such a state where they needed to laugh at the prospect of child sexual assault and the amputation of arms and legs from unexploded bombs. This was a slice of humble pie à la mode.

As hard as it was to see these scenes played by child actors on a stage, I was to encounter real-life dramas up close that affected me even more. The existence of unexploded devices is tragically all-too-normal in Southeast Asia. While traveling to Siem Reap to see the unbelievably astounding ancient Cambodian city of Angkor Wat, I allocated an afternoon to visit the **Cambodia's Land Mine Museum and Relief Center.**

The museum was founded by Aki Ra, one of thousands of former soldiers forced to serve in the Khmer Rouge army. Drafted at age ten, Aki Ra was made to plant tens of thousands of land mines throughout the Cambodian countryside. As he grew into a teenager, he developed a specialty as an explosives expert, known for his calm demeanor and steady hands.

As he entered adulthood, Aki Ra escaped from the Khmer Rouge and used his training and knowledge of where the bombs were buried to begin detonating and clearing landmines. For several decades, he has been removing landmines—more than 50,000 so far.

In addition to removing the mines he and his fellow child soldiers planted, Aki Ra started the Land Mine Museum to tell his personal story and inform the public about the horrors of landmines and the explosive remnants of Cambodia's civil war. The Relief Center cares for forty children and adults, victims who have been wounded, handicapped, or orphaned because of exploding mines.

I stayed for more than three hours at the museum, trying to understand the depth of this problem and learn about myriad explosive devices. One of the most informative exhibits was a mock mine field that teaches visitors how to avoid stepping on mines. For instance, when walking off road, avoid land mines by stepping on places where they can't be easily planted, such as large rocks, dense clumps of grass, or the roots of larger trees.

Aki Ra is appropriately very protective of the children under his care, so you can't meet them, but you can help the children by sponsoring their education or providing basic necessities. While I was visiting the museum, I noticed a Wish List tacked to the wall. On the list was a request for thirty pairs of flip flops for the Center's children. For $75 I was able to purchase all the young children at the Center a new pair of rubber sandals. I figured this was the least I could do.

My trips to the circus and land-mine museum made me think about how young the victims in Cambodia are. The pre-teen girls that become child prostitutes in order to help support their families. And the young boys who lose a limb as they run into a rice field to retrieve a ball. I mourned for the innocence of these children. The fact that they were not growing up in a safe environment and how we, living in more developed, less desperate countries, take for granted the ability to protect our children.

It's this annihilation of innocence, along with the lack of food and inadequate shelter that truly breaks my heart when I think about the people I've seen living and suffering in poverty. The teenager cherishing his one broken shoe. The angry villagers living on the banks of a dirty river. The child circus performers who are miming horrific memories and warnings.

These images are tangled with the memory of the Ethiopian man, wandering the muddy road deranged and naked. Of women balancing cherished blankets on their heads and empty boxes of rubber gloves that could save a life. Of the sounds of croaking frogs and crickets that in my mind now create a symphonic feast.

It is these images that have stayed with me, these memories that bloat me with a deep knowledge that just when I think I couldn't possibly eat even one more piece of humble pie, I will get served another slice.

Chapter 3: **AWE**

My dream of combining my passion for travel with the opportunity to give back was continually renewed by the people I met on the road. Individuals who embrace ideas and ideals, who have conviction and courage, who live with purpose and with passion. People like Yudit-Sensei in Jerusalem, my friend and Himalayan mountain guide Nirma, and Dr. Luther on the Mosquito Coast. I am, quite simply, in awe of these individuals.

There is a generosity of spirit that unites these three, fed by a determination to overcome personal adversity that is honest and intimate and revealing. I strongly believe it's what you do during the tough times that defines your character. Meet these individuals, who not only survived sexual violence, crushing poverty, and endemic discrimination, but learned to harness their hardships, so that others could have better lives.

Yudit-Sensei – Jerusalem, Israel

For a solo female traveler who often finds herself in precarious situations, I can be incredibly nonchalant about my own safety. So before setting out on my extended travels, I decided I would learn how to defend myself. I signed up for **IMPACT**, an assertiveness and self-defense training program geared toward preventing interpersonal violence. It turns out I underestimated both the long-term value of the training, as well as the class' immediate physical and emotional demands.

Our class had twelve students, all females between the ages of fourteen and fifty-three years of age. There was one mother-daughter team, several students, a lawyer, a nurse, a belly dancer. All of us had been physically abused, sexually harassed, or had stalkers. Several had taken out restraining orders against men from past relationships. Half of the women in the class had been raped.

Like all IMPACT instructors, our teacher had survived a sexual assault. She was assisted by two female assistants, also survivors of violence, and two men dressed in suits of full-body armor. Throughout the three-day course, we were continually overpowered in real-life scenarios that forced us to react to violent situations. We learned psychological and physical survival techniques, including how to fight to save our lives. It was exhausting.

I left the training each Sunday physically bruised and emotionally weary. As a group, we women were reliving each others' physical attacks and confronting our collective fears.

I myself had survived several attempted muggings. In both incidents, I had been attacked by my assailants from behind, so my training was tailored to include assaults I couldn't see coming. In one particularly frightening drill, my attackers slipped a bag over my head and I had to fight my assailants without sight. I admit, it took a few seconds to overcome the shock at having been blinded. I needed to first quiet my terror before I could summon the strength to fight back.

For those in the class who had been raped, the scenarios were especially frightening. Their rapes were re-enacted in order for the women to use their new defense techniques to repel their attackers and, most importantly, change the outcome of what had happened. As the training progressed each week, each and every one of us turned into a fighter.

Without a doubt, my IMPACT training was the most empowering experience of my life. Before the class, I had thought of myself as an empowered woman. I graduated from a women's college, worked for women's rights, owned my own business. Yet the IMPACT training took my feelings of self-confidence to a new level. It was exactly what I needed before I headed out on my extended international travels.

Not a day goes by that I don't call to mind the techniques that I learned. I replay them in my mind while walking to the beach, meeting a friend for dinner, entering an empty parking lot, riding an elevator, or while sitting in a parked car.

I found the training so life-changing that I donated two scholarships so other women could benefit. The first scholarship went to a woman from my San Francisco Bay Area chapter. The second scholarship was designated for a woman from one of IMPACT's other eleven chapters located throughout the U.S.

That month's Donate my Dollars poll listed the competing IMPACT chapters and the one that garnered the most votes, received the second scholarship. The Los Angeles chapter won, netting 360 out of a total of 866 votes cast.

To promote the charitable competition, I posted a video of my training and a description of the IMPACT program. Amazingly, the Jerusalem chapter of IMPACT—Yudit-Sensei's martial arts studio—read about the competition and invited me to visit their organization *El HaLev* in Israel. El HaLev, which means "To the Heart," teaches martial arts and self-defense training to women, children, seniors, and people with special needs.

So during the month of July during the first year of my trip, I traveled to Israel and spent a week consulting with Yudit-Sensei and her team. We worked together to formulate business development tactics and ways to promote and expand IMPACT teachings among diverse populations living in the Middle East. Through these meetings, I learned all about El HaLev's important work.

I was especially interested in their program designed for Ethiopian Jewish, or *Bet* women, who had recently immigrated to Israel. The Bet population was having a difficult time adapting to Israeli culture, which is very different from life in Ethiopia. As the men became disaffected, the Bet women were paying a high price through increased levels of domestic violence.

The organization also offered courses specifically for young Muslim women living in East Jerusalem and for individuals confined to wheelchairs. I can clearly recall Yudit-Sensei demonstrating how a person with severe disabilities could use evasion techniques and cause harm to their attackers by biting.

Another highlight during my week at El HaLev was seeing the KidPACT program in action. KidPACT is a four-week summer school providing martial arts training and personal safety tips to girls between seven and twelve years of age. While specifically designed for children growing up in conflict areas, the focus on teaching awareness, self-confidence, and self-protection are life skills that are valuable to all women, no matter what our age.

Each day while working at El Halev, I would take a break to peek in at the KidPACK class. I was thrilled to see girls at such an early age learning to set boundaries and defend themselves by raising their voices and using their newfound strength. That month the Donate My Dollar poll raised enough to fund two scholarships, shared among four girls, allowing each of them to attend the special summer school session.

I thoroughly appreciated volunteering at El HaLev and especially enjoyed meeting the women who worked there, including its co-founder and executive director Yudit-Sensei. This woman is a true force, with a third-degree black belt in judo. She volunteers as a Special Olympics judo referee, she is a survivor of rape and sexual abuse, and is a mother of five.

What's most remarkable about Yudit-Sensei is that she comes from a family of means and doesn't have to work. Yet instead of living a life of leisure, she chose to use her inheritance to open El HaLev. Toiling tirelessly, she personally provides self-defense training not just in Israel, but around the world. Yudit-Sensei has dedicated her life to helping those who are vulnerable learn how to defend themselves.

Yudit-Sensei's sacrifice comes from a place of true altruism. She intimately understands the injustices in a world where women who are physically weaker are often preyed upon and overpowered. In my mind, Yudit-Sensei named her studio appropriately: To the Heart. She is the one who is sharing her heart. I not only admire and respect her ability to overcome personal adversity, but also her decision to dedicate her life to helping others survive.

Nirma Rai – Pokhara, Nepal

My friend Nirma has also dedicated her life to helping others overcome adversity. She helps women climb the world's tallest mountains.

Born in the *Khumbu* region of Nepal, Nirma grew up in a mountain village situated high in the Himalaya and in the shadow of Mt. Everest. Nirma's tiny hillside hamlet is a six-day walk to the local bus station. (And we're talking a Nepali six-day walk, which is a ten-day walk for most other mortals.) From this rural bus station, a seven-hour bus ride takes you to Nepal's capital Kathmandu.

Although she grew up in a typical Himalayan village, Nirma's upbringing was anything but common. First, the eldest daughter of simple farmers, Nirma attended school. Second, excelling early in her classes, Nirma's teachers advanced her age on her official records to enable her to skip several grades and learn at a pace more attuned with her intellect. Third, upon graduating, Nirma won a scholarship to attend **3Sisters Trekking**, an all-female guiding company.

3Sisters Trekking works in partnership with **Empowering Women of Nepal (EWN)**, a nonprofit teaching disadvantaged Nepali girls to become mountain guides. Mountain guides in Nepal, known as *sherpas*, are legendary for their strength and mountain climbing skill. It is a domain traditionally reserved for men.

I came upon 3Sisters Trekking while researching Himalayan trekking companies. Once I read about the all-female guiding teams and the social empowerment work of their sister nonprofit, I knew this was the expedition outfit for me.

Nirma led our team of four young Nepali women porters (guides in training) and four of us foreign trekkers. We had all independently signed up for the twelve-day hike to one of the Himalaya's most pristine spots: Annapurna Base Camp, known in climbing circles as ABC.

I had chosen to hike to ABC because there is only one way to get there: via the Annapurna Sanctuary route. I had heard that the climb through the Sanctuary was most beautiful in springtime, when the surrounding rhododendron forest is in bloom. I was anticipating a lovely hike on a flower-strewn trail.

The description of my trek was enticing:

> **Annapurna Sanctuary:** A classic walk right into the heart of the mountains. This popular trek ascends through picturesque villages to the center of the Annapurna range offering dramatic mountain scenery. Standing in the middle of the Sanctuary, surrounded by towering snowy peaks of up to 26,200 feet (8,000 m), is a truly awe-inspiring experience. Sunrise and sunset are magical as you watch the sun dance on the peaks of Annapurna 1, Annapurna South, Annapurna 3, and Machappuchare. The maximum altitude reached on this trek is 14,435 feet (4,400 m) at Annapurna Base Camp. The trail up is often steep and the Sanctuary trek is perhaps one of the more challenging of the teahouse treks.

I was so excited I neglected to fully comprehend the implications for the phrase "the trail up is *often steep* and the Sanctuary trek is perhaps *one of the more challenging* of the teahouse treks." This seemingly innocuous description coupled with the fact that Nepalis tend to soften bad news, meant I was in for one hell of a hike.

Several days into the trek, I started to decipher the true meaning of Nirma's mountain guiding instructions. For instance, she would say: "The trail tomorrow will be a little bit up," which meant you were going to experience copious amounts of pain. Here's a translation of Nepali trekking speak:

- Gradual Up = Legs will begin to shake
- Little Bit Up = Sweat will pour from your ears
- Up Up = Lungs will be on fire

I have a video of Nirma, in her gentle way, lying to me about the climb ahead. It would be "more than 500 steps," she says with a giggle. I didn't appreciate her humor at the time. Yes, it was more than 500 steps. And 500 more. And 500 more. And this was only Day 2. In fact, the entire trek was a repetition of "little bit up," followed by "gradual up," followed by lots of "up up." I think the real goal was throw up.

Was it worth it? Totally. Even during the final push where heavy snow blanketed the trail. We plunged ahead on that final ascent, breaking trail up to our knees and skittering across ice crystal-covered avalanches. We reached our ABC destination after one of our longest days on the trail and rested overnight. At sunrise the next morning, we hiked the final meters to the highest spot of our journey, an outcropping surrounded by sheer cliffs.

As we stood on this precipice at the break of dawn, we were first enveloped in mist. Then the rising sun burned through the thin air, revealing the most impressive mountains in the world. Here we stood in the center of the Himalayan range encircled by dizzying snow-covered peaks. It was majestic.

And reverent. Colorful primary-colored prayer flags flapped in the wind, juxtaposing the harsh whiteness and reminding us of the sanctity of the spot. Each of us, at first regaling in our triumphant climb, soon became subdued, silently absorbing the immensity of this unforgettable place.

We stayed on the mountain plateau for only about twenty minutes because of the cold. Yet those twenty minutes are some of the most memorable of my life. Offering me a perspective that is only gained through unbelievably hard work, an unfettered belief in oneself, and true teamwork and companionship. It was an awesome experience.

Equally amazing was my new-found love of the yak, which in its various forms helped us struggle up the mountains. The nak, a female yak, produces milk that is turned into a tasty (if slightly rubbery) type of nak cheese. On good days, our hardworking muscles were rewarded with nak cheese pizza. Pretty tasty when you're famished and can't look at another serving of *daal baht*, the local staple of pickled vegetables, curried lentils and rice.

Unfortunately, about half way through the trek, my body started to reject daal baht in a big way. We also ate lots of *momos* (dumplings) and curried fried potatoes—as many as 12 potatoes each during a single lunch break! We were hungry gals, burning lots of calories on our journey "up up" the mountain.

The yak also helped us once we got off the trail for the night. The weather in the Himalaya is always unpredictable and we witnessed some pretty intense storms. Rather than stocking up in Kathmandu, I chose to support the local communities we were passing through and buy my warm clothes on the trek. Along the way I picked up a woolly sweater, a favorite multi-hued hat, and yak-knit booties. When worn all together, I was more than 75% yak! Thankfully I left this look on the mountain.

Another way we got warm was to take bucket showers. For a small fee, a large pot of boiling water could be delivered to the outhouse, offering a chance to rinse off the sweat and grime of the trail. But there was one small hitch...the water was often too hot to bathe in, so you need to mix in colder water. The water we used to moderate the boiling water was the existing bucket of water already in the outhouse. Yes, toilet water. I'm not sure why we thought it was OK to bathe in toilet water, because frankly the idea now seems disgusting. I'm going to blame that lapse of judgment on the altitude.

But the hike wasn't all eating momos, lounging in yak-wear, and toilet-water showers. There was also drinking. While raksi, the local moonshine, was readily available, I stuck mainly to tea. In fact, it soon became apparent why hiking the Himalayas is referred to as the "tea house trekking." Not only are you stopping frequently to warm up and rest with a nice cup of ginger tea, but you are also staying at isolated little tea houses perched high along the mountain ridges.

We were never more pleased to catch sight of our tea house than the day of the big storm. While it rained every day in the mountains, this storm featured torrential rain, complete with golf ball-sized hail, lightening slicing through the sky, and booming thunder. For the first time, we cut our hiking short, choosing to wait out the storm in one of the smallest guest houses of our trek.

Hikers, guides, porters, hosts—about twenty-five of us piled into the one-room house. With steam wafting off our damp clothes, we huddled around a large wood-burning stove in the center of the room clamoring to get warm. While the storm raged outside, I pushed aside thoughts of our wooden shack sliding off the mountain. Instead I snuggled beneath the yak blankets, cradling my cup of tea and chatting with my friends in the warmth of the cozy fire.

With us as an eager audience, it was during this ferocious afternoon that Nirma told us of her historic attempt of the mighty Annapurna IV, a 24,688 foot (7,525 m) peak. The 11th tallest mountain in the world, Annapurna IV had never been climbed by a woman. So 3Sisters Trekking decided to sponsor the first female summit of the mountain, choosing their star pupil Nirma to lead the team of female climbers.

In preparing for this historic climb, Nirma and her three climbing teammates, all 3Sisters guides, traveled to Italy to receive mountain climbing training on the stunning peaks of the Dolomites. Nirma also traveled to Poland to received advanced ice climbing training. These overseas trips meant that Nirma was traveling the world, when more than half of Nepali women can't even read or write.

During that rain-soaked afternoon, Nirma regaled us with the exciting story of her team's groundbreaking summit attempt. The climbing team of four women were joined by a team of four Nepali men with previous experience climbing Annapurna IV. Together they would attempt history as the women sought to become the first female climbers to scale the intimidating mountain. The expedition merited national significance, as the team sought to have a first ascent by Nepali nationals documented in the record books. National pride was on the line for the all-Nepali team to succeed, especially after decades of sherpas helping other nations claim climbing trophies.

After establishing a base camp and taking time to acclimatize, the team set out for the summit in May 2011. Yet before they could conquer the peak, the team was forced back by inclement weather. The group of eight returned to their camp and hunkered down, waiting on the conditions to clear and hoping for a chance at a second attempt. Finally, days later, the weather lifted and the team was given a window of opportunity. The eight climbers set out again. "This time," said Nirma with her quiet smile, "We made it to the summit."

Yet the joy was short-lived. As so often happens in the merciless Himalaya, the weather changed abruptly and the conditions worsened. On the way down the climbers were hit by an avalanche and the entire team was buried under several feet of snow. Amazingly, the eight climbers were still tied together and were able to dig their way out. Miraculously, everyone survived.

While the climbers had cheated an icy death, they had lost all communications. The expedition supporters back at base camp, witnessing the avalanche from far below, had no way of knowing whether the team was alive or dead. The entire nation, including the climbers' families, heard that an avalanche had struck. Their long wait for news of their loved ones' survival lasted several days.

Nirma credits the survival of the entire climbing team to a special blessing they received from His Holiness the Dalai Lama. During a Buddhist ceremony before their historic attempt, the women climbers were given white silk scarves that had been blessed. The scarves were meant to protect the climbers on their quest and they wore them during both summit attempts. Nirma is convinced that it was these delicate pieces of white silk that saved her life and the lives of her friends.

Nirma proudly showed us her sacred scarf during a visit to her home. We had formed a close bond during our Himalayan trek and several of us climbers elected to stay for a few days in the laid-back lakeside town of Pokhara upon our return. Nirma's invitation for us to visit her home was an honor and we eagerly accepted the invitation.

Nirma lives with her sister in a one room apartment with bathroom facilities outside. She has a one-burner flame stove and two beds. The entire apartment was about 12 square feet (3.6 sq m) and was decorated with posters on the wall and family mementos. We saw precious photos of her family, newspaper clippings of her historic summit, her hard-won degree from school, and her climbing training certificates from Poland and Italy. She also showed us her treasured passport.

As we sat primly on the edge of her bed, Nirma served us Nepal's famed butter tea made from the bounteous nak. To me, the tea tasted like an extra-salty cream of mushroom soup. While politely refusing refills, I held onto my cup taking small sips. I'm usually pretty good in these situations and I would never offend my host, but the pungent greasy tea was hard for me to keep down. Nirma noticed and took pity on me. After refusing several more refills, she simply took the cup from my hand, still half full, and ended my suffering.

My reasons for remaining in Pokhara were two-fold. Not only was I in need of a little R&R, but I has also arranged to volunteer with EWN. EWN, founded by the three Chhetri sisters: Lucky, Nicky and Dicky, is the nonprofit arm of their 3Sisters Trekking business.

EWN's goal is to encourage Nepali women to be independent by providing education and job training, which is vital in a country where at least 40% of the nation's 29 million people live in poverty. Compounding the problems of the poor is the country's entrenched caste system, the fact that there is no mandatory schooling, and little healthcare. One of the poorest countries in the world, destitute women and throngs of Nepali children live on the streets.

EWN has helped more than 1,000 women over the last 10 years by providing Trekking Guide Training, where young girls are taught mountaineering skills, knowledge of the nation's flora and fauna, and first aid. In addition, the coursework emphasizes basic English, Nepali history and culture, hygiene, and nutrition. The girls also endure tough physical training.

EWN helps girls from rural regions throughout the country, concentrating its recruitment in West Nepal, a ragged region in an already disadvantaged country. Here girls are particularly vulnerable to child labor, sex trafficking, abuse and abandonment due to poverty and illiteracy.

While my volunteer work with EWN centered on fundraising consulting, I was thrilled to help the organization in other ways. First, 15% of the fee I paid to 3Sisters Trekking for the guided trip to ABC went to support to EWN. My fellow trekkers and I also donated almost all of our trekking gear to our young porters, including back packs, hiking poles, boots, fleeces, jackets, thermals, shirts, hiking pants, hats, gloves, and socks. The gear was in addition to the much appreciated cash tips we gave each young assistant.

I consider myself fortunate to have found the 3Sisters / EWN program for my Himalayan trekking experience. It was great to be guided by such well-trained women during the heavy hiking up the Himalayas and back. This unforgettable experience was marked by the surreal beauty of the mountains, the physical exertion of a hard twelve-day trek, and the life-long friends I made.

Most important, I was able to meet a woman who inspired me beyond belief. The adversity that Nirma faced early on in her childhood was met with a steely determination and sharp intellect that defines her character. Nicknamed the "Laughing Goddess," Nirma climbed to the top of the world, and she did it with a smile and gentle "up, up" encouragement.

Dr. Harry Castillo Luther – Honduras

My friend Dr. Harry Castillo Luther offers another form of encouragement through his work in inter-cultural medicine, a phrase he coined. I was introduced to Dr. Luther and his work through *The Birthing Project USA*, a former consulting client of mine, which provides African American women with pre- and post-natal care. They also support Dr. Luther's work in Honduras, so my friend Kristin and I traveled to the sea-side town of La Ceiba on the Mosquito Coast to meet Dr. Luther in person.

Dr. Luther kindly picked us up after a rocky ferry ride, known locally as the Vomit Comet, and took us back to his house, where he prepared a delicious breakfast of fried plantains, queso fresco, and refried beans. While dining al fresco in his backyard, it was over the breakfast table that he introduced us to his community: the Garifuna.

The Garifuna, with an estimated population of about 600,000, live on the Caribbean coastline, spanning the countries of Belize, Guatemala,

Honduras, and Nicaragua. Historically, Garifuna were West Africans forced into the slave trade and brought to the Caribbean islands of St. Vincent, The Grenadines and Dominica. Once on the islands the West African slaves intermarried with the Carib, the indigenous people of the Americas, as well as the Arawak, the indigenous people of the Caribbean, creating a unique Garifuna identity.

Demonstrating a heated rebelliousness, the plantation owners found it easier to simply deport the troublesome slaves instead of trying to subdue them. The Garifuna eventually resettled Central America's eastern seaboard, including the stretch known as the infamous Mosquito Coast. Named after the Miskito Indians, the region is notorious for its impenetrable jungle, and lack of roads and infrastructure of any sort.

The Garifuna have endured, but not thrived, in this isolated territory. An estimated 72% of the population is thought to be illiterate or semi-illiterate. There aren't enough schools in the area or enough trained teachers. Those who are educated usually complete 3rd grade, while an even small percentage obtain a 6th-grade education.

The Garifuna also suffer poor sanitary conditions and physical health due to a lack of medical clinics, illness prevention programs, and nutrition within the community. Some studies show that nearly 78% of the children under 12 years of age suffer from malnutrition. And 3 out of 10 Garifuna children die before they are 2 years old.

Against this sober backdrop, Dr. Luther's achievements are accentuated. He is the first person from the Garifuna community to receive a medical degree, receiving his education and medical training in Cuba from the Latin American School of Medicine.

Dr. Luther isn't only a trained medical professional, but also a social activist. Understanding the profound healthcare needs of his people, he took action. In 2007, Dr. Luther opened the **First Garifuna Hospital**, the only hospital in Honduras to offer free consultations and medicine. To date, his hospital has treated more than 12,000 patients. And he's seeing results. Health indicators show a decrease in infant and maternal mortality, as well as decreasing pathology from chronic diseases such as hypertension and diabetes.

Despite this early success, keeping the hospital open is difficult. It's especially challenging to find medical staff to care for patients in the isolated region. Dr. Luther's answer is to develop a two-year training program for local women, who study to become auxiliary nurses and midwives. Each time a woman receives her certification and become a nurse practitioner, she is, like Dr. Luther, empowering not just herself but the community she knows and understands.

Another Dr. Luther brainchild is the development of a holistic medical approach called inter-cultural medicine. Inter-cultural medicine not only treats the patient's symptoms, but also the underlying causes of the ailment.

For instance, strained back muscles are a common injury among Garifuna women, and among women in many developing countries who need to carry heavy bundles of wood for the fire. As part of the treatment for the her strained muscles, a doctor traditionally prescribes pain medication, as well as two weeks of rest with no heavy lifting, allowing time for the muscles to heal. But a woman with eight children, an average number in a Garifuna family, is unable to follow this treatment plan. Without wood she can't cook, so how will her children eat?

An inter-cultural medical approach addresses both of these maladies. At the First Garifuna Hospital, the prescription would include medicine for the back pain, rest, and an additional item: a solar stove. The woman no longer needs to cut and carry wood, her back has the opportunity to heal, and her day has many more hours of precious time to devote to herself and her family. This simple example demonstrates Dr. Luther's comprehensive approach to medical care.

But the solar stoves have yet another benefit. Not only are they environmentally-friendly and a cost-effective alternative to open-air cooking fires, they are assembled in the local community. As a result, the production of solar stoves is helping to form a new cottage industry and create employment opportunities in a depressed area. The inter-cultural medical approach that treats the woman's health problem from a holistic viewpoint also incorporates and benefits the entire community. Now that is a radiant glow.

Even from my vantage, I could feel the enveloping warmth of invention. In just a few hours my eyes had been opened to a whole new world. I was deeply impressed by Dr. Luther's work and his personal achievements. I was also inspired by his willingness to forego a more lucrative career as a private physician to provide free medical care to his own community. And I was perhaps most appreciative of his dedication to promoting the idea of inter-cultural medicine so that under-served populations around the world could benefit. The full circle of light that one man can bring to the world is positively illuminating.

The warmth of my hosts around the world never ceases to amaze me. Dr. Luther welcomed me into his home, and fed me—both my belly and my mind. These are the types of experiences that I cherished most during my journey: the opportunity to enter the lives of passionate and purposeful individuals and to hear first-hand their stories of shining resilience. These are the stories that inspire me to keep traveling and to keep giving back.

Whether it's a battered beginning, entrenched illiteracy, or grinding poverty, I have met those who found the strength not just to survive, but to marshal their lives with creativity, conviction, and compassion. I was lucky to find such inspirational people living in the bustling city of Jerusalem, high in the Himalayan mountains, and along the sweaty Mosquito Coast. I was fortunate to have unbridled experiences of wonder and awe.

Chapter 4: **FEAR**

I often get asked if I was ever afraid on the road. My answer: Not as much as I should've been. My biggest fault while travelling solo around the world was an absence of fear.

Part of this is my personality. I'm a natural born risk-taker, not daunted by the unknown or thoughts of personal danger. Another part may just be one's instinct for survival. If you're truly in danger, you don't have time to be afraid. If your fear is suppressed, you can act.

And I seem to have gotten pretty good at suppressing my fear. I can recall quite clearly that during my most frightening moments, my voice drastically changed. It was constrained, slightly garbled, and gruff. I remember thinking that while I didn't actually *feel* afraid, I must be terrified because I didn't recognize my own voice. I had ingested my fear.

While I concentrated on swallowing my fear, those back home didn't put up the pretense. My closest friends and family were pretty much afraid the entire time I was gone. And they had reason to be.

Hector – Zambia-Malawi Border

My first time traversing a border on foot in Africa was more than five years ago, crossing back and forth between Tanzania and Kenya and Uganda. That had been a dodgy experience. But I was so much smarter now. So I embarked on a solo bus trek across Zambia to Malawi.

On this journey, I was traveling from Livingstone, in western Zambia, to the capital Lusaka, then across the eastern end of the country to a small border town called Mchinji, on the Malawi side. I was going to meet a woman who was working with a local NGO. From Mchinji, I would venture to the Malawi capital of Lilongwe and then head up to Lake Malawi to scuba dive. That was the plan.

My itinerary consisted of a multiday bus ride and at first, things seemed to be going pretty well. That was, until I reached the capital Lusaka. As we were approaching the main bus station, taxi drivers started to swarm the bus picking out their fares through the windows. As the only foreigner on the bus, I was creating quite a stir and the bus hadn't even stopped yet.

As I got off, a fist-fight broke out over who was going to drive me to the hotel. The biggest bully won and he was the one who grabbed my bag. I wasn't so keen to get in his cab, but bus stations can be dangerous places and I wanted to get the hell out, so I jumped in the back and asked him to take me to my hotel, asking first to stop at an ATM so I could withdraw cash. This was probably not a good move.

I could see him looking at me in the rearview mirror, sizing up his chances of success if he decided to abduct or rob me. His chances were high, even by my own calculation. But I think my stupidity softened him. It would be like taking the lamb to slaughter. What fun is that? Surely there would be biblical repercussions from such a brute show of force.

And so he decided to spare me and delivered me to my hotel, an international chain, where I cut a half-price deal at the front-desk with my recently drawn funds. Did I give thanks for escaping this close call? Nah. But I did give him a big tip—about $5. I figured my life's worth that much.

The next morning, I hired a reputable taxi from the hotel to drop me off in the pre-dawn hours to catch the border bus which would be making local stops. These local buses aren't as safe as the larger buses plying the international route, but I was aiming for the small town of Mchinji, so it was the local bus for me.

Before we pulled out of the station, food and trinket hawkers streamed endlessly up and down the aisles selling oranges and bread for the trip, small bags of candy, sunglasses, and newspapers. This is fairly common. But on this trip we were joined by a parade of pastors plying the aisles, bibles in hand.

These various men of the cloth would stand up at the front and raise the bible high in the air, preaching to us bus passengers, and praying for our safe travel. I thought this was a whole lotta hoo-ha, but as I looked around, many of my fellow passengers were listening and praying out loud. The pastors were also making a bundle as they passed the hat. I maybe should have been concerned why so many prayers were needed for this journey. But no.

As it happened, I was seated next to a nice young man named Amadeus, like the composer, who was returning home to visit family during his school break. Turns out Amadeus was a huge action movie buff and kept asking me questions about Sylvester Stallone, Arnold Schwarzenegger, and Jean-Claude van Damme, who I quickly pointed out was not American.

Amadeus told me he liked the directness of Americans. Actually, I think his exact words were: "That's what I like about you white people—you just tell it like it is." I found him rather frank himself. Amadeus got off a few stops before my destination of Chipata, on this side of the Zambian border. I was sorry to see Amadeus go. As it turns out, he might have enjoyed the action.

See, the reason I was getting out of Zambia, where I'd been doing volunteer work in Livingston, was because of expected violence in conjunction with the upcoming elections. One of the nuns I'd been working with said she was nervous that there were going to be riots. And when a nun gets nervous, I get nervous.

And she was right. Things were starting to heat up. I'd seen the trucks overflowing with angry youth, fitted with loud speakers that were blaring political slogans around town. And this was in sleepy Livingstone, not even the capital. By the time the bus reached the eastern Zambian border town of Chipata, the crowds were even more animated, wearing opposing political colors, and openly fighting in the streets.

I could see the scene was quickly getting out of hand. There was a mob of protesters, perhaps as many of 100, clogging the street and cutting off the bus route. With no way forward, the bus turned left down a side street, away from the milling masses. But not before the throng encircled our coach and started banging on the sides of the bus. The metal shell started to reverberate with the impact and the noise was deafening. With no way out, I simply closed the filthy window curtain and shrunk down in my bus seat, hoping to avoid detection.

Luckily, our driver remained calm and slowly but surely we made our way through the detour, finally arriving at a small dirt bus station several blocks from the mob. Once at the station, I quickly looked for a shared taxi to the border. It should've cost me 20 Kwatcha (about $4) to share a taxi with four others. But there was no one else heading that way, so the taxi driver wanted to take me downtown to pick up additional fares. Instead, I insisted that he take me straight to the border without heading back towards the chaotic city. We negotiated a private taxi fare for the equivalent of $8, I climbed into the front seat and we set off in the direction of the border.

Except it wasn't a private taxi ride as promised, as I found out when we stopped at the gas station to fill up the tank for the trip to the border. It's actually fairly typical in African countries that your fare will help pay for the fuel. But this time, as we prepared to pull away from the gas station, four young men joined me in the cab.

Turning to the taxi driver I started to argue loudly, telling him I had paid for a 'private' taxi but he just kept telling me to calm down. Instead of calming down I reacted, opened the car door and jumped out with my small backpack. Luckily we hadn't yet picked up much speed and I was able to land on my feet. He stopped the car in the middle of the road and he and his buddies got out and started yelling at me.

Suddenly my IMPACT training kicked in, and I started yelling back, wanting to create a scene that would draw people's attention. The driver was screaming at me to get back in the car and I was screaming at him to give me my backpack out of the trunk. All the time I was aware of the threatening sounds of a political mob throbbing only a few streets away. It was getting pretty animated and I was on the verge of walking away and ditching my bag when he and his buddies finally threw my bag out of the trunk and got in the car, congratulating themselves on taking my $8. I grabbed my bag and walked down the sidewalk to a grocery store that I had picked out as a safe spot before pulling out of the gas station.

By now I was pretty desperate to get out of this exploding town. I sat outside the grocery store steadying myself before deciding to hire yet another cab. This time I gave the taxi driver $10 as I attempted another private ride to the border.

As I got in the front seat, my driver introduced himself as Israel and told me the name of his tribe. This was a very formal introduction and put me at my ease, knowing his family name and his standing in the community. He was about fifty years old, with a bit of grey hair, and a very calm manner.

Israel drove me the 5 miles (8 km) to the border, chatting with me along the way. As we approached, he rolled up our windows and locked the doors against the onslaught of touts that lie in wait around the immigration station, preying on those of us braving the border on foot.

Israel told me to walk directly to the immigration building and that he would bring my bag to me so I didn't have to endure the menacing touts any longer than necessary. I did as he said, hoping that he would bring my bag over to me as promised and not simply drive away. But

Israel was good on his word and thanks to his help and kindness, I passed through Zambian customs without incident. I walked the 500 yards of no-man's land between countries, making it to the Malawi border.

Greeted by the inevitable crowd of young taxi drivers vying for my business at the deserted border post, I had no choice but to take my chances again. I negotiated a ruthless $35 (one month's salary) to drive me less than 3 miles (5 km) into town. My driver took me to the one hotel in Mchinji ($9 for a room with a private bath!), where I stayed for the night. I immediately tried to connect with my Malawi contact. Unfortunately, she was not in the border town as planned, but in the capital Lilongwe. The next day I was back on a local bus.

The hotel was located just on the outskirts of town, so all I had to do was stand along the dirt road and flag down a minivan, or *matatu,* as they're called in Africa. I hopped in the first one, which turned out to be a bit of a mistake. You see, choosing your matatu is like selecting a piece of fruit. You want one that's looking fresh, one that's not too bruised on the outside. I didn't adequately inspect my matatu that morning and it turned out to be battered goods. But too late. I settled in for the one-hour ride.

About two hours into the drive, we were stopped by a police road block and asked to pay a fine. They wanted around $18 – $1 per person in the van. Unfortunately, my matatu driver didn't have the money to pay the bribe, so they waved us over to the side of the road where we waited another hour sitting in the hot, stifling van.

At this point, the police had started to get frustrated with our inability to produce the pay-off and we were told to drive to the police station.

Here, still sitting silently in the matatu, parked in front of an Old West-style police station, we waited for another few hours. Things were looking glum.

Finally our driver was able to borrow the needed funds from someone on the other end of his cell phone. I'd considered paying the fine hours earlier, just so we could be on our way, but I didn't want to be seen as being flush and was curious to see how long we would actually have to wait. The answer: more than three hours. We were saved by a little girl with pigtails who produced the compulsory $18 from a pocket sewn on the front of her gingham dress.

After three straight days on numerous buses I had fallen into a bit of a stupor. To survive bus travel in Africa, one must enter a zen-like state and completely let go of any expectations of on-time, safe, or comfortable travel. You must embrace total acceptance of the unknown. Of course, I may have entered this transportation trace, not through an elevated mental state, but through simple dehydration. But whatever. At this point, I didn't fully care.

About a half-hour of traveling back on the main road, I was shocked out of my narcosis. We had stopped to pick up passenger #19, a distinctly singular dude. He freaked me out because he had some crazy eyes and was wearing an animal fur hat, Daniel Boone-style. Except I think it was hyena fur. I later learned it was the hat of a Zulu warrior. Also, he had a machete.

As we made predictably slow progress along the deeply rutted road, our new addition kept talking loudly to no one in particular. And while I didn't understand him, I don't think his comments were particularly complimentary to me because my fellow passengers kept giving me sympathetic sidelong glances. Did I mention he was carrying a machete? My only consolation was that he was two rows back, so if he wanted to slit my throat, he'd have to lean over an entire row of people to do it.

The matatu chugged along until six hours later it stopped altogether. The three guys in the front seat got out to push and managed to jump start it. At least the first couple of times. But then the bus truly wouldn't budge. The solution was to lift the front seat off and start banging with a hammer until there was smoke. This bit of strong-arming did the trick and we slowly crept our way into Lilongwe. Bruised fruit indeed.

Putting on my cloak of invincibility, I marched past the taxi stand and jeers, lugging my bag with wheels through the mud. I'd noticed a respectable looking hardware store a few blocks away. It was here that I asked the kind owners to call me a cab. I had no hotel reservations and my trick of negotiating a cut-price deal at the fanciest hotel in town didn't work. In the end, the cabbie and I drove around for about an hour before I found a decent hotel for $10 a night called the Golden Peacock. Nirvana.

I settled in at the Golden Peacock, meeting with my Malawi contact. I started to size up the city and, like neighboring Zambia, Malawian politics were starting to get hot. These clues told me I wasn't in the best place:

No Tourists: I usually find myself off the beaten track, so this doesn't always alarm me. But in Lilongwe I met a fellow traveler, who told me that he was the only tourist coming from the Mozambique side, where I was heading. And when I stopped at a tour agency to enquire about group tours to Lake Malawi, thinking safety in numbers, the agency told me there were none. No tours and no tourists? No good.

No Economic Necessities: When the country starts to run out of vital necessities, it's alarming. Here in Malawi, there were troubling shortages of foreign exchange both at Barclays and on the black market. There was also no fuel, and most disconcerting of all, no Coca Cola. As in "the local Coke manufacturer can't get the ingredients to make its secret addictive Coke recipe." Now, I think the world may very well be coming to an end when you can't buy a Coke. Seriously, this freaked me out the most.

Evacuated Aid Workers: I was still sticking to my plans to make my way to Lake Malawi to scuba dive until I met an aid agency worker shaving her legs in the communal bathroom. It was the first running water she had seen in a while and she was pretty excited at the prospect of being evacuated to Johannesburg. She advised me that if I was going to stay in Malawi, it was best not to go outside at all during the next few days, but instead to hunker down and wait for the political rioting to pass. Hmmmmmm.

I discussed this dilemma with my new best friend Hector, who I met in the driveway of the Golden Peacock. Hector is in his 70s and was walking with a cane. Originally from Cuba, he's a nurse living with his wife outside of St. Louis, Missouri. He said he was looking for a new hotel because his $8 room didn't have a fan and he wanted to upgrade. I told him the Golden Peacock did indeed have fans and that it was very nice. (Did I mention the running water? Swank!)

I kept running into Hector, in the lobby and on the small patio attached to the guest house. We were hanging out swapping stories and road tips as travelers do. I was trying to go overland to Mozambique via Lake Malawi, where he'd just come from, and he was trying to get to Livingstone, where I'd just left. I told him about the rioting I'd seen and advised another border crossing. His own multi-day overland excursion from Mozambique made my recent Zambian crossing seem like a piece of cake.

Starting his journey in South Africa, Hector had gone to the Johannesburg bus station to buy a ticket to Mozambique. Upon completing his transaction, he asked the ticket agent where he could find a taxi. The salesman pointed him to a young man and told Hector to follow him, which he did.

Now the young man kept walking a ways ahead and Hector had to hurry to catch up, barely keeping the young man in his sights. Suddenly, he made a sharp turn and Hector followed into the alleyway. Only after he'd already entered the side street did his sixth sense kick in.

Someone jumped him from behind. Hector felt hands round his throat strangling him and then he lost consciousness. When he woke up several minutes later his money belt and wallet were gone. Luckily, his muggers were professionals. The thieves knew how much pressure to put on Hector's wind pipe to cut off his air supply, but not to kill him. And they cradled his head during his fall, so his skull didn't crack open. Did they do this out of kindness? Probably not. I think a murder charge weighs more heavily than a robbery charge, so it was probably more about self-preservation. When he awoke, some vegetables sellers sitting a few feet away pointed to Hector's passport, lying in the gutter where his assailants had tossed it aside.

But here's the thing. Hector's money belt and wallet were decoys, with expired credit cards and very little cash. His real money was ingeniously stitched into a secret lining in his pants. Hector was very proud of his invention (which he designed and sewed himself). He drew me a diagram in my notebook while we sat on the patio one afternoon. Respect!

Eventually, the situation in Lilongwe demanded a decision. I had to make a choice to hunker down with Hector and ride out the impending riots or flee the country. We both decided to stay a few days, then take our respective buses heading in opposite directions out of the country. This would allow me to visit Lake Malawi and do some volunteer work I was looking forward to in the countryside.

So Hector and I stocked up on supplies: water, fruit and breakfast bars, as well as extra phone cards and internet access cards. We were prepared to ride out the storm. But after a few Skype calls with family and friends frantically asking why I was staying, I decided to change my plans. Honestly, I think they heard my husky (scared) voice and knew that the situation in the capital was dangerous.

After sleeping on it, I realized that I didn't have to "hunker down." This wasn't my country and I'm not a journalist reporting the story for the world to witness. Yes, I'm trying to do good work along the way and I was very much looking forward to volunteering in the countryside, but I'm essentially just a tourist. I'm choosing to be here. And I decided that I could choose not to be here.

I broke the news to Hector early the next morning about my plans to fly to South Africa. I urged him to come with me, but he had no desire to revisit the country of his mugging misfortune. In the end, Hector stayed and tried to get out via the same bus station I came in at. I later found out he couldn't leave and he got stranded at the Golden Peacock, eating the breakfast bars and fruit I left for him.

By this point I was on my way to the airport, set to fly out on the morning of the scheduled protests, with the streets already filling up. There was only one seat left on the last flight out to Johannesburg and they were asking a hugely inflated $1,000 for the one-way, 30-minute flight. To reserve my seat, the airline representatives were demanding cash. (All the easier to skim a few bucks off the top). I found the only working ATM in the airport and was amazed that it continually coughed up the dough I needed to secure the last seat.

Collapsing into my seat, I started to release a bit of my pent-up exhaustion. I thought about why I was so set on staying in Malawi and my decision to finally leave. In the end, I concluded that I could have an adventure anywhere. I didn't have to be in a place that was deemed so dangerous that international aid agencies were evacuating their field personnel. So I swapped scuba diving Lake Malawi with a pony trek in the stunning Kingdom of Lesotho. It was a good trade.

While my solo bus travels and border crossing gave me great moments of concern, they also gave me a glimpse of the real Africa, where many of the countries are still evolving as modern political entities. This is one of the reasons why I love Africa—you get to witness the transformation that's taking place. It's a continent that is constantly changing, where every sense is heightened, and around every corner is a new encounter. It's a place where you come face-to-face with your ignorance, affording you the opportunity to not only learn a great deal about the region, but also about yourself. I just wish that I didn't have to learn my lessons the hard way.

Charles & Roger – Beirut, Lebanon

The warmth and generosity of the Middle Eastern Arab cultures is beyond the pale. Truly I have never had so many people open up their homes to me. I was honored to be a guest in their lives and their countries.

This hospitality was particularly evident in Lebanon, one of the most complex countries I've visited. On one hand, you have Beirut, the cosmopolitan capital, complete with a seaside corniche, trendy restaurants, high-end shopping, and colorful street performers. I'll never forget walking to dinner one night and passing three well-dressed men with bandages across their noses, telltale signs of their recent date with the plastic surgeon.

On the other hand, Lebanon offers a glimpse of a timeless rural life that still exists throughout much of the Middle East, complete with ancient medinas, leisurely lunches, and endless afternoons filled with coffee and conversation. In this flashback to more simple times, the tranquility of the countryside is punctuated only by the sounds of singing birds and the Muslim call to prayer.

I was invited to Beirut to work with **This is Baladi**, an organization dedicated to preserving and promoting Lebanon's heritage by encouraging youngsters to learn about their country's cultural diversity. Children who participate in Baladi's field trips learn about the rich texture of their country in a fun and interactive way, using food and the arts to promote and foster a sense of collective belonging among the country's youngest generation.

Baladi's work has another important benefit, in that it helps to build harmony among the countries' confessional and religious divides. Aiming far beyond simple tolerance of cultural and religious differences, Baladi's inter-cultural excursions are considered a model in helping to rebuild unity in post-conflict countries such as Iraq and Sudan.

I spent several days volunteering with Joanne Bajjaly, founder of Baladi, and my fellow consultant and friend Inji, whom I had met years earlier while volunteering in Cairo. We were discussing new ways to generate revenue and assessing new avenues for organizational growth.

While staying in Beirut, Inji and I shuttled between our apartment in the city's center and Joanne's home in the suburbs. Here, on Joanne's balcony overlooking the sea, we three women collaborated to find new ways to expand Baladi's social business model.

One of the advantages of meeting in Joanne's apartment was the chance for me to see a modern Middle Eastern lifestyle up close. Joanne lives with her extended family in a stylish apartment that has sweeping views of the Mediterranean. I got the chance to meet and dine with her charming husband, her mother, and her children.

Equally fun was a follow up two-day tour of Northern Lebanon with Baladi guides Charles and Roger. Joanne had arranged for this 'taste of Baladi' as a thank you for volunteering my time and traveling to Lebanon to work with her.

During our personalized tour, I got to taste the varied terrain of Lebanon: mountains, wet lands, seascapes and cities, and visit each of Lebanon's diverse populations: Sunni, Shiite, Maronite Catholics, Druze and Bedouin. Until this insightful tour, I had no idea the variety of landscapes and how culturally rich Lebanon is as a country. Which is exactly the point Joanne and Baladi are making.

The tour was fantastic. Roger and Charles led the way, each of them taking great pride in their home country. Roger, an avid basketball fan, enjoyed both educating and coaching the children during their camps. Charles, a trained historian and Francophile, is an ardent

Arab nationalist, raised in the Maronite Church and reader of tarot cards. Charles actually looked a bit like Yasser Arafat, particularly when he was wearing his *keffiyeh,* the iconic Arab scarf.

Charles and Roger were two complex individuals living in a complex country—just like us all. I was safe in their hands traveling, and yet I'll admit, I still got pretty nervous a number of times during our road trip.

Part of this tension resulted from reminders that the country's ongoing political strife is never far away. For instance, before leaving on our adventure, I encountered several unsettling incidents in downtown Beirut:

After dinner one night, as Inji and I were walking back to our apartment, we heard a series of loud shots. We were uncertain if the noise was fireworks or gunshots or an incoming missile. We took cover under an apartment overhang, just to be on the safe side.

While strolling through the winding streets, Inji pointed out the main headquarters of Hezbollah, a Shi'a Islamic militant group and political party based in Lebanon. I kept my head down and eyes averted as we walked past the guards stationed outside.

Driving to meet a potential donor, we made it through the city's usually crammed streets in record time. Why was traffic so light? Because there was a Hezbollah bomb scare. Why were we on the road? No idea.

One evening while on the balcony I notice a white car with its hood up, parked just outside the apartment building. I immediately think of the movie *Blackhawk Down* and wonder whether this is a signal for an imminent attack. I check to make sure there's no 'X' taped on the roof of the car. There's not and I wander back into the apartment for a glass of water.

Only slightly unsettled, we left the bustle of Beirut for my personalized tour of the Lebanese countryside. The entire two days were exhilarating, giving me an eyeful of this fascinating country. Charles and Roger showed me a side of Lebanon that you don't hear about in the news.

We visited the Bekaa Valley, hiking through this biblical landscape and admiring the picturesque scenery and abundance of birds. At the tail-end of our hike, we came across an itinerant Bedouin family living out of a wagon. The mother was cooking over an open fire, while a small boy played on a tire swing not far away. It was here in the Bekaa that we also visited a Druze temple. I donned an obligatory robe and quietly entered the place of worship, joining the silent men and women in prayers.

We also visited Mount Lebanon, the highest mountain in the Middle East. It still showed patches of snow even though it was summer. We traveled the winding road up to the top to appreciate the setting sun from this high vantage. The next day, we strolled through Lebanon's ancient cedar forest, spying the actual tree adorning the country's flag.

The night before we spent in a Maronite Village and took the morning to feast on local delicacies and visit several ornate orthodox churches. Lebanon retains a distinctive Maronite character, with almost a quarter of its people attending church and practicing this strict orthodox faith. The sanctuaries we visited were nestled deep in the mountains, with meditation caves carved into the surrounding mountainside. Here, monks seeking solitude, would cut themselves off for private prayer and reflection.

One of the last stops on our tour was Tripoli, the country's second largest city. With a large Sunni majority, Tripoli's women wear *abayas* and head scarves. It was here that I had the best meal of my entire two-year trip, a hand-made feast full of lively mint and lemon flavors. I followed Charles and Roger to the popular restaurant, hidden deep within the city's medina. After walking the endless corridors, we found ourselves in a delightful spot brimming with local hospitality and stuffed ourselves with regional ambrosia.

During this dizzying tour, the one time I was worried was when we were visiting the Roman ruins in the town of Baalbeck, a known Hezbollah stronghold. On the outside walls encircling the ruins, there were large revolutionary posters and patriotic songs blaring from loud speakers. Surrounding this tourist spot were yellow and black flags adorning every street lamp, signaling Hezbollah territory. Further up the road, a flag featuring the Hezbollah patriarch and Syrian President Assad was flying outside the Lebanese Army barracks, a clear indication to the army that they were not in control of this region. Looking around me, they were right. The Lebanese army was certainly not in control of this part of the country.

It was here in these unsettling surroundings that we got lost. Each time we stopped to ask for directions, I cringed, not wanting anyone to notice me, an obvious foreigner, sitting in the back seat. During my time in Lebanon, there was a series of renewed threats of foreign kidnappings throughout the Arab region in retaliation for Bin Laden's killing. We eventually found our way, but for a girl that doesn't usually perspire, our unscheduled side trip made me sweat.

This last incident is a perfect example of the complexity that characterizes much ofthe Arab region. While we were lost in Baalbeck, we stopped at a fruit stand to ask the way. The fruit merchant gave us a handful of plums to enjoy as we continued our car ride through the countryside.

So while I felt some fear, I also felt an amazing generosity. This is the duality that marks this complex region. And not just for travelers like me, but more importantly, for the people who live there. It must be an incredible strain to live your life tempering your fear while enjoying the abundance and goodness around you. I think it would be exhausting.

The Kogi – Ciudad Perdida, Colombia

During my travels the person who experiences the most fear, wasn't me, but my mother. Only now am I realizing the strain I put my family under as I went off gallivanting around the world. While I was out having adventures, my loved ones were at home, not having nearly as much fun.

I tried my best to keep my friends and family informed. For instance, I sent Mom a detailed spreadsheet every few days with updates on where I was going to stay and how I was going to get there. Unfortunately, many of the columns were filled with generic descriptions like "public bus from Cartagena to Santa Maria." Not only did my mother not know where these places were (she did generally, but not specifically), but she was left with the knowledge that I was taking public transportation around Colombia which was, and remains, under U.S. government travel warnings.

During the last six months of my trip in South America, I was actually paying closer attention to government travel warnings. My radar was up mainly because I was beginning to feel disbelief that I had made it through the trip relatively unscathed. I was starting to get the inkling that my number was up, my luck running out. Not a good feeling to have.

So while I tried, the system I had for keeping my loved ones informed was imperfect. This never became too much of a problem, until one of my updates didn't get through. As luck would have it, this occurred in Colombia, known for pervasive hostage taking.

The U.S. government had deemed the corridor between Bogota and Cartagena safe for Americans to travel, taking normal precautions of course. And I stuck to these parameters when touring the country. Almost. That is I stuck to them until I decided to venture just a tad south of this safe zone in order to head into the Colombian jungle.

I felt I had good reason to ignore the government travel warnings. I wanted to trek to the famous *Cuidad Perdida*, Colombia's Lost City. I had heard much about this iconic trek and exploring these ruins was actually one of the reasons I had come to Colombia.

The five-day hike covers about twenty-seven miles and is considered moderately difficult, with lots of steep ascents, some bouldering, and only a small jungle path to follow. I relied on a sturdy bamboo walking stick, given to me by my guide on the first day to help me stay upright on the muddy, slippery slopes.

Hidden in the country's southern Sierra Nevada mountain range, Ciudad Perdida is a pre-Colombian city that was founded nearly

650 years earlier than Machu Picchu. The city was thought to have been abandoned during the Spanish Conquest in the 1500s, and was only rediscovered again in 1972 by local treasure hunters who began finding gold and ceramics in the surrounding area.

When the government became aware of the selling of these historic artifacts, they sent a team of archeologists, geologists, and biologists to unearth the ruins. In 1976, the Colombian government declared Ciudad Perdida to be a national treasure.

Since then, anthropologists have discovered a tiled network of roads and three central circular plazas, accessed by an entrance atop 1,200 stone stairs. They've also found evidence of how the city functioned, with markets, an administrative center, and alters for religious ceremonies. I particularly love the simplicity of Ciudad Perdida. You can see that people lived here long ago.

This paradise is anchored by three central terraces that stand out, discs of vibrant green, against the surrounding hills tangled in vegetation. Banana trees, bamboo, and cocoa plants grow wild and are cultivated throughout the lush jungle landscape. These crops are guarded by men in camouflaged fatigues.

I greeted them with a nod as I walked by wondering on which side of the conflict they stood. The armed men could have been Colombian government forces, or guerrillas representing the Revolutionary Armed Forces of Colombia (FARC), or the National Liberation Army (ELN). They could also have been a private guard of a coca lord.

I decided not to dwell on the circumstances since the situation was entirely out of my hands. I mean, I was already there. If we were to be kidnapped, the men with machine guns would do it. We were at their mercy. My trademark nonchalance was firmly intact.

The trek included quite a number of river crossings. Some were just small streams, where we took off our shoes and scampered across. Others were fairly deep and we took off our pants and waded through about thigh-high. On the return trip home we were getting lazy and either hitched a ride on the backs of our guides or simply splashed across without bothering to remove our boots. I was actually hiking in sneakers since I'd given my boots away to Nirma back in the Himalayas.

One of the highlights of the trek was at the end of the second day, when we visited a waterfall with several of the local children. The water was spectacularly cool and refreshing after a long walk in the jungle heat. We ripped off our clothes and spent hours jumping off the rocks and swimming around in the crystal clear water, laughing and playing games.

Our path also took us through several small indigenous villages. Native Colombians call this area *Teyuna* and it's populated by tribes who believe Ciudad Perdida to be the center of an intricate network of villages. Unlike some, our trekking company was on good terms with one of the tribes, the *Kogis*. I was fascinated to visit a Kogi village and see their way of life up close.

During the day, all Kogi adults are off working in the fields, leaving the smallest children to be looked after by a few older ones. Both Kogi girls and boys have long hair and wear long tunics, so the only way to tell them apart is the side-slung bag worn by boys and the long beaded necklaces of the girls. These Kogi kids were full of mischief. Playing hide and seek, spying on us, shyly accepting the small gifts that several of the trekkers brought to share. At night, some of the women would visit our camp, eating with us, and selling hand-woven bags.

While I've seen my share of ancient lost cities, including Peru's *Machu Picchu*, Cambodia's *Angkor Wat*, and the Mayan ruins at *Tikal* in Guatemala, the stark fact that you can only get to Colombia's Ciudad Perdida via an arduous five-day hike makes the trip all the more compelling.

Though the trek was immensely satisfying to me, it was not so enjoyable for my mother. See, upon arriving in Taganga, the small seaside town that is the jumping off point for the hike, I learned that the trek was being closed down for the indigenous full moon ceremonies. It would be closed for two weeks, so if I wanted to go, I had to leave the next day. No brainer.

That night, I loaded up on a few supplies, including a local black soap that was supposed to keep the mosquitoes at bay, and dashed off an email to my mother letting her know that I was leaving for the trek a few days earlier than expected and I'd be radio silent in the interim. Unfortunately, she didn't get the email.

That meant the last message she'd had from me was that I was taking a public bus along the Colombia coast outside the American safe zone, and that I would contact her when I arrived safely. Since she didn't get my email update, she didn't hear from me for several days, and she started to worry.

And she had good reason to be fearful since my route took me into the heart of the Colombia drug wars. Two groups of rebels, the FARC and the ELN, have been waging a guerrilla war for more than forty years. Both groups operate freely in the region, which is widely considered unsafe, and both groups routinely take hostages.

During the height of Colombia's civil war in the 1990s, the FARC alone kidnapped at least 2,500 civilians. Typically, guerilla organizations demand a ransom, while paramilitary groups generally use the practice of hostage taking as a means of terror or coercion. The most notorious kidnapping of tourists occurred during this same trek to Ciudad Perdida in 2003, when 8 trekkers were kidnapped by the ELN and held for 101 days.

Following this incident the trail was shut down for a few years, but has since re-opened and tourists have started to trickle back. When I was there in the fall of 2012, the area was experiencing another surge in kidnappings and as I write this in June 2013, I heard another group of foreign trekkers were taken while hiking along the same exact trail.

So Mom had reason to be concerned. First, she focused on news from Colombia, which wasn't good, since it was covering a story of two foreign women who had been recently kidnapped. Second, she turned to the travel spreadsheet and looked up my lodging to try and track me down. Luckily I'd updated it right before the bus trip. Enlisting the help of her neighbor, a former Spanish teacher, she called the hostel where I was supposedly staying and learned that I had indeed arrived and had set out a day earlier than expected.

Mom was relieved, but angry. The moment I walked back into the hostel, exhausted, muddy and hungry, I received a message to call my mother. Boy, did I get an earful! And an ultimatum that I had heard at least twenty times before: "It's time for you to come home."

But for me, it wasn't. I was fresh off a fascinating trek to see pre-Colombian ruins in the heart of the jungle! I got to meet an indigenous tribe of people I didn't even know existed! It was exactly the type of adventure I was looking for. No fear on my end. And, callously, not much sympathy for those back home either.

Operating without fear isn't recommended when travelling abroad. Fear helps sharpen our defenses. Fear helps keep us from venturing in too deep. Fear helps stop us from our own stupidity. In retrospect, if I could've benefitted from one thing during my two-year trek, it would have been a healthy dose of fear.

Chapter 5: **JOY**

To me joy is an unexpected delight. A discovery that makes me giggle, catch my breath, emit a tiny scream. Joy is intoxicating, contagious, and fun. It is the true definition of happiness.

Scientists believe that one experiences joy when living the good life. Basic needs are met and you're able to explore and embrace the world around you. It's the opportunity to flourish.

I was able to flourish—to thrive—in the least likely places. The thick interior jungles of Uganda, an empty salt plain in Bolivia, and a tropical island in the Caribbean. Actually finding joy on a sultry island does make some sense. So let's start there.

The Three Amigos – Bay Islands, Honduras

I met my friends The Three Amigos: Astrid, Greg and Kristin, while volunteering on the island of Roatan, part of the Bay Islands, about 30 miles (50 km) off the eastern coast of Honduras. Known for its diving, the reef off Roatan offers 73 species of coral, including Staghorn and Elkhorn corals, 41 species of sponge and 185 species of fish. A marine bounty!

Roatan Marine Park exists to protect all these glorious marine resources, trying to create a sense of environmental responsibility and promoting the idea of conservation on this exquisite island. Like me, Astrid and Greg were consulting with the organization. They were spearheading a responsible seafood campaign to educate locals and tourists about food safety. My volunteer workshops focused on how to fundraise in the U.S., while Kristin was helping the group out by painting buoys. So that's how Astrid, Greg, Kristin and I started to hang out together.

I had no definite plan when I arrived on the island, but after about a year on the road, I found myself dropping anchor for two whole weeks. At that point, it was the longest time I had stayed anywhere. In addition to the volunteer work, I was deep sea fishing, sea kayaking, and scuba diving with my new friends. So much fun!

Since I was on a travel hiatus, I took this opportunity to get my advanced diving certification, enabling me to deep water dive, wreck dive, and night dive. It was during my first night dive that I saw one of the most beautiful sights of my life.

It was a moonless night, when there was little or no light filtering through the water, and we dove deep down to the ocean floor. When we turned off our flashlights, we were in complete darkness, floating weightless in the black ink. Spooky.

Kneeling on the sandy bottom, we waited for our eyes to adjust to the lightless depths. Gradually, the phenomenon known as the "String of Pearls" began to appear. A universe of tiny flickering lights in the blackness all around us. It was like sitting in the middle of the Milky Way, with twinkling white Christmas lights everywhere you turned—breathtaking!

The String of Pearls is only found in very warm waters around the world. The "pearls" are bioluminescent semen from tiny crustaceans used to attract females during mating. Each string of semen is specific to a particular crustacean, just like our human DNA.

Most evenings, after a day spent either volunteering or diving, I would join Astrid, Greg and Kristin for happy hour on the roof deck, where we would toast the setting sun. Late into the night, we would work very hard at perfecting our guacamole and rum drink recipes.

It was during one of these impromptu parties that Astrid and Greg convinced Kristin and me to leave the island to explore the Honduran jungle. We readily agreed, packed our small backpacks, and took a ferry to the Honduran mainland, heading inland to a mountain lodge on the *Rio Cangrejal* (Crab River). The Rio Cangrejal is absolutely stunning, bisecting two national parks.

One of the lodges in the area is run by an organization called *Guaruma*, a nonprofit organization which teaches the youth of the river valley about eco-tourism, conservation, and sustainable land use. Students train as trail guides, maintain the trails, and speak out on ecological issues. Most important, the students become role models in their community and are starting to lead local conservation efforts.

Unfortunately, I didn't get a chance to stay at Guaruma's lodge, opting instead for another locally-owned lodge a few miles down river. There in the jungle hide-a-way, we amused ourselves with a host of fun activities, such as horseback riding through the jungle and along jade-colored streams and mountain biking down windy dirt roads and through friendly, flower-lined villages. We also indulged in river-side picnics, one in full view of a natural waterfall that served as an outdoor shower for the village's young men. Sumptuous views all around!

During our rural bike ride, we stopped to visit a local women's co-op in the village of El Pital. The cooperative taught women the skill of sewing, while providing accommodation for those seeking refuge from violence.

Unfortunately, Honduran women suffer one of the highest rates of domestic violence in the world. In fact, the second highest cause of death for Honduran women is domestic violence. I was appalled to learn that at least one woman a day dies at the hands of her husband or boyfriend.

The El Pital refuge was started in an effort to provide local women an opportunity to earn a living and thus achieve independence. To help protect the battered women, the co-op and refuge are located on the far side of a fast moving river, a deep gorge separating the women from their abusers. To gain access we sat inside a large metal basket, each of us taking a turn hauling the basket via a thick wire cable connecting the two banks. We pulled the basket along hand-over-hand, high above the churning river below.

It took quite a bit of muscle to work the pulley system. But it was worth it. Our little mountain biking group toured the refuge then browsed the items for sale, each of us purchasing non-essential items like pillow shams, shoulder bags, and pot holders in support of the women's job training. It was lovely to connect with the women and see them building a life for themselves in a very small village, in a very dense jungle, in a faraway place.

Back at the lodge, after all the fresh air, exercise and river-side shopping, our Honduran parties continued. We ate all meals under a shaded canopy, with a slight breeze stirring the air.

After dinner every night we headed to the bar to taste the local moonshine called *guaro*. Distilled from sugarcane, this homemade liquor comes in a bottle filled with marinating leaves and twigs. And that's just what it tasted like—leaves and twigs. Actually, in my mind, *guaro* is suspiciously close to the spelling of *guano*, which means "shit." I kind of think the locals were having a joke on us by charging an outrageous price and making us do shots made with scraps from the forest floor.

One of the reasons we came on this mountain adventure was to go whitewater rafting. As a veteran of Class IV and Class V rapids, I was being a bit of a snob and wasn't sure the Rio Cangrejal was going to be gnarly enough for me. But I was wrong. That river almost killed me.

Our first day of rafting was fairly benign, so on the second day we convinced our guide to take us into the more advanced whitewater. The top section of the river was amazing with tons of top-level rapids and plenty of heart-pounding rushes. It was fun! That is, until I saw my life flash before my eyes.

Coming out of an early rapid, I gripped the top of the paddle and pulled hard, toes dug into the seams of the raft to try to hold on and keep balance. But Kristin and I just weren't strong enough to paddle correctly through the current.

We went down the fall sideways, boomeranging out of the whitewater toward a rock wall. It looked at first like we were going to simply bounce off and head back into the rapid, but the rock wall was actually a granite overhang with just enough room for the raft to slide under.

At the last moment, our guide yelled "limbo!" which I guess was a command to lean back on the raft, like you're undulating under some bamboo pole at a Hawaiian beach party. But that instruction didn't compute for me. It wasn't one of the commands we'd practiced just minutes before.

While Kirstin and the guide leaned back, my instinct was to lean forward. Unfortunately, I couldn't get as flat and the rock overhang cleared my skull with mere inches to spare. It all happened in a split second and when we emerged I looked back and saw our guide looking a little gray. Deep into the jungle, there was no medical help of any kind. To be evacuated would mean a three-hour jeep ride on a gutted dirt road.

After all the rafting excitement, I was particularly looking forward to my siesta that day. There were a number of hammocks strung up along the perimeter of the patio for me to choose from. The one prized hammock in the shade was already taken. And the hammocks tied to trees meant you had to keep on alert for the red ants that trailed down the tree trunks. So in the end, I chose the hammock under the open air cantina.

I was having a grand siesta, reading my book and cat napping. Every now and again, I'd reflect on my harrowing brush with death on the rapids and congrat myself on being alive. Later that evening over a glass of stick shit, one of our river guides casually asked me how I could sleep so peacefully with a boa constrictor over my head. Whatttttt?

Yep. My chosen spot for a siesta that day was also the favorite berth of the resident boa constrictor. Sure enough, I went back to the cantina and looked up. I saw a giant snake situated high in the rafters of the open-air hut, right above my hammock. Not cool.

The next day I thought I could do it again, be brave and take my siesta under the boa constrictor. After getting myself settled in the hammock I looked up and—surprise! No snake. Now the only thing worse than seeing a six-foot snake, is not seeing a six-foot snake and knowing that it's in the vicinity. Truly frighting.

I tried to shrug it off and tough it out. I ain't afraid of no snake! But alas, I couldn't do it. Images of the coiled creature kept popping into my mind every time I shut my eyes. I retreated, opting instead to risk the biting red ants.

Now, you may be wondering why these experiences made it into this chapter entitled "Joy." I mean, who would really think that swimming with semen, surviving a near-death experience riding the rapids, and sleeping with a six-foot snake would constitute total and utter elation? Me. Although you might be right to question this self-styled definition of happiness.

Julie & the Llama Fetuses – La Paz, Bolivia

Bolivia is a country that strips away all preconceptions and really gets under your skin. That's why I call it "Mind-blowing Bolivia."

For example, Bolivia is the only country in the world with a law which accords nature the same rights as humans. This law presumes that

Earth is a collective entity of public interest and specifies Mother Earth's life-systems, including human communities and ecosystems, as having inherent rights that need to be protected. Too cool!

This is also a country that likes to party, and night after night you'll see Bolivians dancing in the streets. Most adults join dance clubs within their neighborhoods, much like the competing quarters in Brazil's carnival. Every evening these dance clubs are out in force, their members practicing for hours. The party-goers dance in lines up and down the street, music blaring. It's quite a social scene, with tons of flirting going on. I would lean out the hostel windows to watch.

Bolivians most like to show off their dance move during street parades. A mainstay of Bolivian life, these parades, along with the food, drink and music, are paid for by wealthier members of a community in a system called *preste*. By paying for parties and parades, the rich earn the respect of their neighbors. Each person dancing in the parade wears an elaborate costume not unlike the sequined outfits that America cheerleaders wear. The parade costumes cost on average $250, a princely sum in a developing country.

Mind-blowing Bolivia is also known for the noteworthy traditional dress worn by the women. Called *Cholitas,* these rural women are distinguished by their pint-sized bowler hats, perched on their heads at a jaunty angle. This was most intriguing to me and I had to find out why in the world they would adopt this bizarre fashion statement as a part of their national costume.

Apparently in the 1920s, a shipment of bowler hats arrived from Britain intended for the colonialists working on the construction of the railroads. The hats that arrived were too small (child-sized really) and they were distributed to the locals. The women seized upon this foreign freebie and the bowler hats instantly became a cultural icon.

The Cholita ensemble is completed by the pigtails worn by grown woman. Cholitas take great pride in their long hair and try to make it appear even longer by adding black yarn pompoms to the ends. Pigtail-extensions.

What I like most about the Cholitas' pigtails is how they are used to advantage in the wrestling ring. One of the highlights of my stay in the capital of La Paz was a fieldtrip to see this unusual form of wrestling. The night I went I was lucky to see the World Cholita Wresting Champion. I even got to have my picture taken with her, World Championship Belt held high above her head!

During the bout, the women pull down one another's many skirts and tug each other's pigtails. The men also fight in costume, outfitted with silver lame capes and Batman-inspired masks. During the match's finale, the fight promoters set the perimeter of the fighting ring on fire with blowtorches. What's not to love about a spectacle of this magnitude? Pure infectious fun!

I enjoyed the Cholita wrestling match with Julie, who I had met that morning at a rather rambunctious hostel in La Paz. She and I were sitting at the bar, eating breakfast and re-charging our iPhones. We struck up a conversation and I invited myself to tag along with her to visit the city's Coca Museum and the Witch's Market.

The Coca Museum was a fairly tame affair, with exhibits about the historical and medicinal uses of cocaine. It featured many exhibits showing how the drug has negatively affected traditional Bolivian life. The highlight was buying some locally made cocaine candies that I brought home to slip into my family's Christmas stockings that year. Nothing like distributing some drugs at yuletide.

The Witch's Market was much more fun. I decided to splurge and update my cold-weather gear with some fetching llama wear, in a happy assortment of rainbow colors. While feeding tourists' need for all things llama, locals come to the Witch's Market to buy shaman talismans, like llama fetuses.

Yes, that's right: llama fetuses. In Bolivia, shamans use llama fetuses as part of their magic rituals. The dried fetuses, hanging by their neck or stacked in baskets, are buried under the front door of Bolivian homes as an offering to the goddess Mother Earth Pachamama. They are thought to help ward off bad luck. Although there doesn't seem to be a whole lotta luck for the llamas in these parts.

During our excursion, Julia filled me in on Bolivia's stunning Salar de Uyuni, part of the region's *altiplano*, a high-altitude desert that was formed along with the Andes Mountains around 40,000 years ago. The Salar de Uyuni spreads out over 4,000 square miles (10,500 km), is surrounded by mountains, contains fresh and saltwater lakes, and features miles of salt flats. It is roughly 25 times the size of the Great Salt Lake in the U.S. state of Utah.

The surface of the Salar is mostly covered with a solid salt crust, ranging from mere inches to a thickness of nearly 10 feet (3 m). These salt plains are all that's left of several prehistoric lakes. In the center of the Salar are several islands formed from the tops of ancient volcanoes, sticking out of the desert salt like icebergs. While devoid of most wild life and vegetation, this rare landscape is unbelievably breathtaking.

I visited the remote and eerie Salar v
in a 4x4, an absolute necessity in these
expedition, we explored the vast blazing
and were astounded by its distinct physic

My favorites were the *Ojos de Sal* or "Eye
glue-like substance on the salt's surface. T\   ,...uicate
that there's water bubbling up through the ...crusted earth. I was
also mesmerized by *Inca Huasi*, translated as "Fish Island," because
of the abundance of fish fossils left over from when the region was
a submerged lake. Fish Island is an oasis of giant cacti looming
in the middle of the salt flats. It is ruggedly beautiful in the stark
surrounding moonscape.

The Salar's high-altitude lagoons include the amazing blood-red
Laguna Colorado, Stinky Lake, named after its sharp sulfur smell, and
Laguna Verde, which changes color from blue to a blinding emerald
green every day at 11:00 am. We also saw three species of pink South
American flamingos which breed there, their glamorous rosy color
the result of the pink algae found in the lakes.

Finally we arrived at the hot springs and geysers named *Sol de
Manana*, or "Tomorrow's Sun." Getting out of the 4x4, I delayed a
minute, fiddling with my camera. Only after running to catch up with
the group and sliding between the bubbling pools of mud did I learn
that the temperature of the geysers was more than 300° F (149° C).
Fall in and I'd be boiled in seconds. This information might have been
helpful before we exited the car and traversed the sulfuric death traps.

Despite dodging scalding potholes, navigating cacti forests, and
surviving blinding sun, Bolivia's Salar de Uyuni was so much more

ed and one of my favorite places in the world. Its
beauty, stark images, and remote location all combine to
it one of the most intimidating and yet intimate landscapes to
plore. It provides an opportunity to climb inside a Dali painting and
marvel at the surreal surroundings up close. Enchanting!

Getting the inside scoop on the Salar was just one of many things
I learned from Julie. I also learned that she was in La Paz to take a
breather from her volunteer assignment on Lake Titicaca. She was
stationed on the highest navigable lake in the world, with a surface
elevation of 12,500 ft (3,812 m), with an environmental organization
called **Sustainable Bolivia.**

Julie was volunteering with the Bolivian Amphibian Initiative and her
job was to collect data on the frogs that live in Lake Titicaca. She spent
months gathering and meticulously recording her data on a computer,
her contribution helping to document Bolivia's rich biodiversity. When
the research team tried to sync up their data with an international
database, the spreadsheets were corrupted and all their hard work
was flushed down the toilet in a nanosecond. All the information was
lost because the organization was using bootleg software.

While Julie had become pretty disenchanted with her volunteer
gig, her husband Josh, was having a grand time working on the
educational side of the Lake Titicaca conservation effort. In his role
as a community educator, he was able to engage the local community
in his work and make enduring changes in behaviors and attitudes
toward environmentalism among the indigenous populations.

When we met at the hostel, Julie was recovering from the loss of her
hard-sought data and spending a few days in Bolivia's big city. As we

played the typical tourists, we chatted, and I discovered this woman is the poster gal of global volunteering.

As an environmental scientist, Julie tends to volunteer with organizations that focus on conservation work. Her first gig was three weeks spent with the Environmental Agency of Iceland working on a conservation trail team in national parks around the country. If you ask me, this sounds like a pretty fabulous way to peruse and preserve Iceland's stunning terrain. Sharing talents and sightseeing at the same time—a true Adventure Philanthropist!

After wrapping up in Bolivia, Julie was heading to the Galapagos Islands to volunteer at the *Jatun Sacha Foundation,* which has a well-organized system of biological reserves. Each reserve has a central station that helps to manage volunteers as they assist with reforestation, environmental education in nearby schools, and the promotion of sustainable agricultural methods. Julie would be assisting with scientific studies on the fauna and flora of the Galapagos Islands.

As a volunteer, Julie would pay about $600 to be able to live and work on the Galapagos for 2 weeks. This is an amazing deal, since a trip to the Galapagos usually runs about $2,500 a week. She would be contributing to important research, while having a great time diving in one of the world's most protected ocean ecosystems. Fabulous gig!

Following the Galapagos stint, Julie and Josh were heading to Cambodia to work with the *Trailblazer Foundation*. The couple originally got involved with the group through her friendship with the organization's founders Scott and Chris Coats, based in Jackson Hole, Wyoming.

Julia and Josh started volunteering with the group locally, helping with several fundraising initiatives that included a stint for Josh as DJ (see every skill is needed!). Now the couple has decided to continue their work with the group in Siem Reap, Cambodia, where they'll be helping build a water sanitization and filtration system for several villages. The clean-water work goes hand-in-hand with a local initiative in sustainable agriculture, micro finance, and health awareness.

While Julie and Josh are helping the organizations they're volunteering with, they're also benefitting from their experiences by:

- Using professional skills to learn more about areas of interest that they love: environmental conservation and education
- Building their work resumes with international projects
- Spending extended periods of time living in and learning about local communities around the world, and
- Exploring the world in an economical way

Julie is just one of the many travelers I met on the road that were living a similar life to mine. All of us curious about the world. All of us extending a helping hand. All of us learning valuable lessons. And all of us having the most joyful time of our lives!

Nshongi Family – Bwindi, Uganda

I encountered joy in another form while visiting the shores of Uganda's Lake Bunyonyi—happy healthy children at school! Situated on the northern banks of the lake, just a short canoe ride away from our campground, is a school called *Little Angels Needy Children and Orphans Project*.

In Uganda, orphans bear a significant disadvantage in terms of their wellbeing and social mobility. A child that has lost one parent is referred to as a "single orphan" and a child that has lost both parents is referred to as a "double orphan." Serving the Bufuka village area, the Little Angels Project cares for 200 needy children between three and eight years of age. All the children are living significantly below the poverty line.

As part of the Little Angels program, the children receive an education, a nutritious meal while at school, and rudimentary healthcare. Orphans are housed with families in the village. The houses have no electricity or running water. Most children don't have a bed, but instead sleep on a mat on the floor.

Little Angels was founded by a young man named Duncan. He told me how he started the school (his second one) as a way to repay the generosity of the donor who sponsored him while he was growing up in rural Uganda. Duncan tells a powerful story of the Little Angels under his care, prompting me to give a small $50 donation on the spot.

I discovered the Little Angels while I was staying at a campground on the shores of Lake Bunyonyi ("Place of many little birds"), only a few hours drive from Bwindi Impenetrable National Park. I was in western Uganda for one reason: to visit the mountain gorillas.

Mountain gorillas are dangerously close to extinction. With only 790 left, mountain gorillas are only found in two places: the Virunga Volcanic Mountains of Central Africa and Bwindi.

Living up to its name as one of the thickest jungles in the world, Bwindi allows only sixty-four visitors a day into the park, charging each person $500 for a permit, which must be secured in advance.

Visitors head into the jungle in groups led by park rangers, gorilla trackers, and an armed security detail of two Ugandan soldiers carrying machine guns.

For the record, Bwindi is the site of an infamous tourist abduction in 1999. At the time, 150 rebels kidnapped 14 tourists and murdered 8 of them. Actually "butchered with machetes" was the exact language used in news reports. I'm not sure what 2 soldiers could do against 150 armed rebels, but let's not dwell on that tidbit.

Each morning, even before the tourists arrive, trackers set out to find the gorillas, which move about the park feeding. Sometimes the gorillas are close to the starting point, sometimes not. Our hike was one of the longer ones—about 4 ½ hours into the thick of it and unsettlingly close to the volatile Congo border.

The park rangers cut a trail with their machetes, just wide enough for us to climb through the jungle, following signs left by the trackers. What made the climb hard that morning was that the gorillas were moving along several very steep mountain ridges. And make no mistake, this is truly the jungle. Within an hour I ripped my pants while lifting my leg up over a log and had to tie my rain jacket around my waist for a modicum of modesty.

Physically, gorillas are a pretty impressive species. Males usually weigh twice as much as the females, at nearly 500 lbs (226 kg). Males can reach a height of more than 6 ft (1.8 m) and can have an arm span of more than 7 ft (over 2 m).

That day, we were tracking the Nshongi family of gorillas, which has twenty-three members, including four adult male gorillas, called silverbacks, and five juvenile males. The family is named after the dominant silverback called Nshongi. After hours of hot sweaty slogging, we finally caught up with the Nshongi family, its members meandering through the jungle and calmly eating leaves.

Adult males are the most aggressive, so when you see multiple silverbacks in the wild, as we were lucky enough to do, you need to be extra careful. When amongst the gorillas, there are several rules to follow. First, you need to stay at least 22 feet (7 m) away and you must limit your visit to one hour. The one hour I spent with the Nshongi was, hands down, the most memorable hour of my life. Simply being in the presence of these amazing creates is absorbing, especially when you look straight into their intelligent eyes, see their facial expressions, and witness their familial interactions.

As an endangered species, there are a number of obstacles placing the mountain gorillas in danger. The loss of habitat due to over-harvesting in the forest and pollution. Human population growth is also encroaching on the gorillas' native habitat as subsistence farmers in the area surrounding the national parks claim the land for planting. Sadly, some gorilla families are becoming isolated as their territories are being divided and signs of in-breeding are starting to appear.

War and civil unrest in the park area are also contributing factors to the destruction of traditional gorilla lands. Poaching is an ongoing problem for the gorillas, not so much for bushmeat, thankfully, but more as a result of gorillas getting caught in the snares meant for other animals. And, unfortunately, there is still a black market for live gorillas which are worth between $1,000-$5,000 to zoos and as pets. Not long ago, a Malaysian zoo apparently "found" five gorillas for their wildlife park.

Gorillas are succumbing to the spread of disease. Although park rangers can deny anyone with a cold or other symptoms from entering the park, tourists bring harmful germs within close proximity to the gorillas. It's thought that 20% of mountain gorilla deaths are due to contracting a human disease.

To spend time with these rare beings in the open jungle is an unforgettable experience of wonder and pure joy. Perhaps the one word for it was "intense." In fact, the entire week I spent in western Uganda could be considered intense—but not always in a good way.

It all happened because I have beautiful feet. Truly. The type of feet where strangers in Italy come up to caress them. The type of feet perverts on the New York City subway compliment. The type of feet that appear in foot calendars for those with a fetish. (No comment.)

So my feet are undeniably my best feature and I appropriately take good care of them. I always have a pedicure and lotion them twice a day. I take pride in their soft smooth skin. As it turns out, my soft smooth feet are also attractive to some other undesirables creatures.

Several weeks before I arrived in Uganda, when I was still at the beach in Mozambique, (remember my birthday surfing lesson on the beach with the breeching humpback whale?) my surf instructor Clayton mentioned that some of the surfers were getting parasites in their feet. They weren't sure if was from the beach sand or going barefoot in the market. Well, since I would never dream of going barefoot in a market, I considered myself and my lovely feet to be safe.

I was so secure that my pretties were safe that I shrugged off Clayton's description of how locals used a sea shell with a serrated edge to cut the worms and their accompanying egg sacks out. Since the parasites enter the foot at their softest part, they usually breed in between the toes. This meant that quite a few people were walking around sans a digit or two, the result of toe amputations.

Several weeks later, while waiting for friends in a bar in Kampala, I happened to look down and saw what I thought was white pus on the sole of my foot. I asked the guy sitting next to me if he thought they were parasites, but he didn't think so. Why I thought this was an appropriate ice-breaker, I'm not sure. When you travel solo for long periods of time sometimes your social skills are off.

But when I asked others who had been in the area longer, they agreed that I had worms. The creepers had embedded themselves in the soles of my feet because they were so nice and soft and swishy. I'd just taken a hot shower (don't get many of those in Africa) and as a result of the steaming water, they were partially emerging. What I thought was white pus, was actually a white tape worm coiled up upon itself. I tried to squeeze or pop it while sitting in the bar, to no avail. Once again, fairly questionable social skills.

So it was clear there was something foreign living in my body and it wasn't good. When my friends arrived, a local Kenyan and a South African, they confirmed the parasite self-diagnosis and agreed the buggers had to come out. At this point, I realized I'd contracted them at least two weeks earlier and time was of the essence before the eggs had time to hatch. My beautiful feet!

But wait. We were all about to head into the jungle to visit the gorillas. The last thing in the world I wanted was an open wound while hiking in the jungle. The risk of infection was too high. So I hatched a plan. I would continue to host the worms for a further three days, until after the gorilla trek, and then I would undergo emergency bush surgery.

Now, bush surgery isn't as bad as it sounds. It only means that you need to perform a medical procedure with household instruments in an un-sterile environment. Ok. Right. It doesn't sound too good. But when you have worms coming out of the soles of your feet, you don't have a lot of choice in the matter, especially when my priority was not to get the worms out, but to see the mountain gorillas. Questionable priorities for sure.

So I went on the trek. Which turned out to be slightly torturous since during those three days, the parasites took on Edgar Allen Poe-like dimensions in my mind. I could practically feel them throbbing in the soles of my feet. It didn't help that I was afraid if I walked strongly I would burst the egg sacks. This was slightly disconcerting.

Now, don't get me wrong, the visit to the mountain gorillas was absolutely worth the mental anguish of living with worms in my feet for an extra three days. But just barely. All the way back from the gorilla trek I was so excited, anticipating the bush surgery to come later that night. It was probably because I was so preoccupied with these joyous thoughts of parasite liberation that I fell into a puddle of elephant pee. And it was a BIG puddle.

The puddle was so big that we had to jump from rock to rock to cross. In my haste to return, I pushed through the crowd and started across only to slip on one of the rocks and fall in. I sunk in up to my knees. That's how big a puddle of elephant pee is. Darn good thing I didn't have an open sore in my foot—yet.

But before the night was over, I would have one. It was Patrick, our Kenyan overland truck driver that did the honors. Our guide, Jay, was tasked with subduing me with whiskey, although he drank most of it himself. And Marco, the guy I first showed my worms to in the bar in Kampala, held the camera and filmed the event for me.

Truth be told, Patrick did a masterful job, using a sewing needle sterilized by me with hand sanitizer, which he promptly wiped with his grease-stained fingers (he was a truck driver after all). I didn't actually see him un-sanitize the needle until I watched the video afterwards. Patrick took the needle and deftly dug the worm—egg sack and all—out of the bottom of my left foot. Oh joy!

The bush surgery video captures the pure elation on my face during the process, the complete and utter happiness that I was finally getting rid of my worms!

I thanked Patrick profusely, bought him a couple of beers and I was good to go. I was heading back to Kampala with the gang, then onwards to northern Uganda on my own. It was here in the town of Lira that I saw a heart-stopping sight: another parasite. Apparently, I'd been so overjoyed with getting the little guy out of my left foot that I somehow failed to notice another parasite in my right foot. True story.

Now it was three weeks since I had been in Mozambique and I was haunted with the thought that the eggs might hatch inside my foot. I needed another bush surgery. Some of you may wonder why I didn't simply go to a hospital, which would be the logical thing to do. Except when you're in the rural region of a developing country. The people at the local health clinic have terrible and contagious diseases like

TB and malaria, and I learned that it's best to stay as far away from a clinic as possible. When we passed by the clinic in Lira, I told the driver to keep right on going.

So, bush surgery #2. This time I enlisted the help of Jacob, a local Ugandan who was employed by the outfit that I was volunteering with. Jacob was game. He had seen these types of worms before and he knew what to do. His surgical instrument of choice was a razor blade, so we bought a few from the front desk at the hotel and he went to work on my foot.

Did I mention that Jacob only has one eye? Yep. I allowed a man with an eye patch who I had known for only an hour to attack my beautiful right foot with a razor. It's called desperation.

Unfortunately Jacob botched it. He cut the head of the worm off (floating around still in my foot?!) and split open the egg sack too. I guess that's what you get when a one-eyed man performs surgery.

The egg sack burst was BAD—one does not want a bazillion parasite eggs let loose in an open wound. And severing the worm's head was also NOT GOOD. He had to go in multiple times with the razor blade to try and find the head because we didn't want it to rot in there. At this point, I'm feeling a bit sick, what with all the butchering of my feet. But I gather my strength and stay the course.

Unbelievably, I waited another four days before returning to seek medical attention in the capital. Once back in Kampala, I went to a "real" doctor, you know, one with a medical degree in tropical diseases and clean fingernails. He was British trained, but the fact that he was wearing a Bugs Bunny tie didn't instill a huge degree of confidence.

He looked at my wounds and said there was no need for me to be alarmed. Apparently, the proper treatment is to remove the parasites at home with a sharp instrument. So both the needle and the razor blade were the proper utensils to use and bush surgery was the right decision. On top of this good news, he found nothing rotting in my foot. Yippee!

Since I was there, I took the opportunity to show him what I thought was a spider bite on my butt. He looked at this itchy red welt on my backside and announced he was "unimpressed." (Did he mean my butt or my bite?) Apparently, it wasn't a spider bite, which he was kind of excited about seeing, but merely the result of a stinging caterpillar that I sat on.

At this point, I prepared to leave Africa. I packed my bag and puddle jumped flights from Kampala to Nairobi to Cairo to Madrid to the small Spanish island of Mallorca to board a ship. My next adventure was to be a Trans-Atlantic crossing from Spain to Panama.

This lengthy cruise gave me an abundance of time to reflect on my recent escapades. The intense wonder of seeing the mountain gorillas up close. The elation of finally having the worms excised from my feet. It was then that I realized that each of us has the opportunity to create our own definition of joy.

And to me, what really stuck in my head was not just the fun I had in each locale, but the friendships that made the experiences richer. Because truly I'm happiest when enjoying the fun with someone— sharing a giggle, an element of surprise, an unforgettable sight. After all I've seen, it's the friendships that stick most in my mind and my solo travel is what made these friendships possible.

The fact that I travel alone has encouraged me time and again to invite others to share a sunset, to introduce myself to a stranger at a bar, and to meet up with friends from another country and caravan across a continent. To me, joy is sharing. Sharing our riches. Sharing our ideas. Sharing our hearts. Just keep the worms to yourself.

Chapter 6: **ANGER**

You may have noticed by now that I'm a girl with a lot of energy; nevertheless I'm fairly even-keeled and slow to anger. That is until I'm confronted with outright injustice and then I see red. I find it particularly intolerable when a certain class of people is discriminated against—women, the disabled, ethnic minorities. I think at the core level it offends my sense of fairness and equality.

There were only a handful of times that I was truly angry during my two-year travels, and all of them had to do with a violation of human rights and innocent people suffering. During my global canvas, I found the most egregious acts in Africa, Egypt, and Southeast Asia.

Jacob – Lira, Uganda

As so often happens, the place where you experience the most joy is also the place that can move you to fury. This occurred during my time in Uganda, after I left the serenity of the mountain gorillas.

While back in the States, I arranged an excursion with an organization helping bring clean drinking water to rural communities in East Africa. I also arranged my largest donation to date. Because I wanted to make the donation participatory, I invited the readers of my GoErinGo.com site to vote on the location of the well. They chose northern Uganda over Kenya and South Sudan—thankfully (although I think my mother and her friends might have rigged the voting with multiple entries).

Unfortunately, once I arrived in Kampala my extensive pre-trip preparations unraveled fast and it soon became apparent that I would need to make my own way. Now, traveling in northern Uganda is dangerous by any stretch—think rogue militia leaders (KONY 2012 / The Lord's Revolutionary Army), child soldiers, mass rape. I was faced with the serious decision of whether I would or would not go it alone to the northern city of Lira.

After much reflection and anxiety and quite a few sleepless nights, I decided to go. I went mainly because clean water is an issue about which I feel passionately. Also, I was already in the country to see the mountain gorillas and I was looking forward to meeting the local community who would benefit from the clean water. Furthermore, since this was my largest donation to date, I was excited to see the funding in action.

After making the decision to move forward I drew up a five-point plan of action to ensure my own safety, which included:

Kidnap & Ransom Insurance: Before I left on my worldwide travels I bought Kidnap & Ransom (K&R) insurance. I knew that I'd be traveling alone throughout Africa and the Middle East and so bought the policy for about $1,200 a year. Individuals can't buy this type of insurance, but companies can. As president of my own consulting firm, I purchased the policy for myself.

Along with the policy, you get access to a personal safety team. I called them before I left the United States to introduce myself, thinking that if they had a voice / face with the name, they might try just a little bit harder to find me if I ever got truly lost. I refreshed these contacts before leaving for Lira, sending a series of emails to let them know I would be traveling in the area, the dates I was traveling, and the name of the host nonprofit organization.

U.S. State Department Registration: I almost *always* register with the U.S. State Department's Smart Traveler Enrollment Program (STEP) before entering a new country. Not only will this alert the U.S. government that you are in the country during times of conflict, it also supplies them with next-of-kin information in case of an emergency.

Private Driver / Bodyguard: I decided not to take local buses like I normally do, but instead hire a driver, who could then serve as a sort of bodyguard for me. I wanted someone who spoke the local language, knew the area, and would accompany me into town.

While in Kampala, I tapped some local friends to help me find a driver, which they did, supplying me with his State ID, Driver's License, and a background check. I hired the 4x4 car and driver for five days for about $1,000, which was a significant cost for me and a princely sum by Ugandan standards. It was worth it though, as my driver Fred was the consummate professional, trained to drive in Germany and incredibly serious about his job. This was exactly the person I wanted by my side.

Personal Emergency Procedures: My family and I have a safe word that I am to use if I'm in imminent danger. If they receive a call or message with this word, they are instructed to call the K&R team, the U.S. State department, and the local embassy. I sent a message to my family to be on alert that I was heading into dangerous territory.

Self Defense Training: As you know, before I left on my travels, I went through the three-day IMPACT self-defense training course. While making my arrangements in Kampala, I took the time to review what I had learned, so my skills were fresh.

Whether or not I needed these elaborate precautions, I felt better knowing that I had taken all the steps I could to protect myself. In the end, I was incredibly pleased with my decision to travel to Lira. It's what the trip was all about: heading into unknown territory to have a more authentic travel experience centered on community engagement.

During my days on site at the well I met many members of the community, talked with women who lived in the village, and gained a greater understanding of their need for clean drinking water. I attended the open–air village church and was treated to the local congregation singing for me in the age-old African tradition.

I also visited the children attending Apache SDA, a boarding school for about 350 students. On my first day more than 200 of the school children took me to see the original water well, which was too shallow and consequently polluted with E. coli. The new well that we were building was to be at least 230 feet (70 m) deep to ensure a clean source of water and was being built on the grounds of the SDA school. The students were very proud to show me around.

The well is now up and running, providing clean water to more than 5,000 people living in four villages. Each family of ten-to-fifteen people uses 26 gallons (100 L) a day: 10 gallons (40 L) for drinking, the rest for cooking, cleaning, and bathing. With a typical water jug holding 5 gallons (20 L), each family needs to make five trips to the well a day just to meet their most basic water needs.

Although I was there the first day for the ground breaking of the well, full construction took about six months. I was especially pleased that while the machinery was European, the drillers and engineers who worked on the project were all local Ugandans.

At the base of the well is a plaque and as the donor I got to choose the inscription. Here's what I wrote:

May your life overflow with possibilities.

This sentiment expresses my wish for all the families using the well. At the very least, I hope that the clean water will help make their lives easier and give them greater health.

This is also what I wish for the students, that they are able to study and have choices in life. With education comes the ability to earn a living and greater opportunities. I hope they grab hold of the options that are before them.

The plaque also speaks to me personally and the possibilities that my worldwide travel brings. The opportunity to travel to northern Uganda to volunteer was a possibility that, despite the risks, I could not pass up. It was a journey that taught me a great deal, not only about the people I sought to help, but also about myself.

See, my trip to northern Uganda made its mark on me, not because of the parasites raging in my feet at the time or the extreme stress of deciding to make the journey solo, but because of the emotional angst it caused.

During my two-year trek, I made more than 65 donations and of these grants there was only one that I felt truly angry about—my donation to build the well in Uganda. A combination of factors made me not quite regret, but certainly rethink, my giving decision.

It took four months of deep thinking for me to understand why I was so enraged. I finally figured out that I was upset because I felt that the nonprofit had broken the implicit promise between donors and organizations.

For instance, during my stay in Lira, one of the nonprofit's in-country staff asked me for money for his personal use. Jacob, the same young man who took a razor blade to my foot, asked me to reimburse his incidental expenses like phone calls and taxi rides. He also invited a friend to dinner and ran up the tab while passing me the bill. After a day of swindling, I took him aside and told him that his actions were inappropriate. He apologized, but his behavior still left a bad taste in my mouth.

Also when I made the public presentation of the award, the head of the community, a pastor, asked me for more money instead of thanking me. Granted it's hard for foreign nonprofit organizations to control the behavior of end recipients, but nevertheless, I was left again feeling fleeced. I also didn't appreciate the jokes about rich American donors. This incident is really a microcosm of the problem with aid to Africa in general and the culture of dependence and expectation it's perpetuating.

Last, while I was still in Lira, I raised my concerns with the founder of the U.S.-based nonprofit because I thought it was important that he knew that I'd had an unsatisfactory giving experience. He promptly apologized, but then called me the next day to say he'd refund my donation since I wasn't happy. He ended the call by stating that his organization didn't need the funding anyway.

Obviously my intention was never to renege on my donation and I had, in fact, already given in full by the time I had traveled to Lira. Yet hearing that my donation wasn't valued was adding insult to injury. This misguided gesture made a bad situation even worse.

Ultimately, I came to see that the founder did me a favor. During our telephone conversation he asked why I was disappointed if the end recipients received the funded project. I gave money to build a well to help rural Ugandans receive clean water. That's where my money went and the villagers were benefitting. So why was I so disappointed?

I thought this was a fair question, and one I hadn't asked myself. In my fundraising seminars, I always talk about the importance of knowing the motivations of your donor. Making a charitable donation is a personal and complex decision. The desire to help others is obviously part of the giving equation, but there are more factors that inspire a person to give.

Up until this point, I hadn't really spent much time discerning my own motivations as a donor. But now, after putting some thought into it, I'm clear about what I expect when I make a donation:

- **Good Work.** I want to truly believe that the organization is helping its constituents and providing vital services.
- **Effective Management.** I want the organization and the donation to be stewarded properly.
- **Funding Need.** I want to give where the donation is needed.

I think the organization I supported in Uganda fell short on the last two motivations for me: effective management and the need for funds. This is why I was angry with the overall donor experience.

As I came to understand the reasons behind my anger, I took steps to channel my ire into something more productive than just hot air. I took the time to think about which organizations I'd been happy to support in the past and why. Two in particular stood out:

Ethiopian Women's Lawyers Association: This organization helps fight for women's human rights. While I spent several days providing pro bono development work, including writing a fundraising plan for the organization, at the time I didn't give a donation. I rectified this oversight by ear-marking a donation to help women and girls achieve equality in Ethiopia.

Lubashi & Lushomo Homes: Based in Zambia, these organizations help provide a home for orphaned children and shelter for girls that have been sexually abused. I initially gave a small grant to these organizations and now substantially increased my donation to help protect and support these vulnerable children.

Today I'm no longer resentful of the situation in Uganda since I've been able to turn my anger into an excuse to do some good. My disappointment with building the well in Lira prompted me to evaluate my own giving motivations. This insight encouraged me to think more about the end beneficiaries of the clean water—the 5,000 villagers—and to more fully appreciate the opportunity to help make their lives a little bit better.

In addition, the examination of my own anger motivated me to make additional donations to nonprofits that I felt were doing vital work on behalf of promoting women and girls' rights and protecting abused children. So what started as anger became opportunity. And hopefully an overflowing of possibilities for those who need them the most.

Rebecca Chiao – Cairo, Egypt

The United Nations General Assembly designated November 25 as *International Day for the Elimination of Violence Against Women*, hoping to raise awareness of the fact that women around the world are routinely subject to rape, domestic violence, and other forms of violence. This is a day for reflection and action toward all the progress that is still desperately needed.

There has been great strides over the last several years to help protect women around the world. For instance, 125 countries now have laws that penalize domestic violence. The United Nations Security Council now recognizes sexual violence as a tactic of war and equality between women and men is guaranteed in the constitutions of 139 countries.

Good stuff, but more needs to be done when globally 6 in 10 women have suffered physical and/or sexual violence in their lifetime. More than 600 million women live in countries where domestic violence is not considered a crime and an estimated 60 million girls are child brides. Nearly 140 million girls and women have experienced female genital mutilation. It's also estimated that more than 600,000 women and girls are trafficked across borders each year, mainly for sexual exploitation. Mind-numbing statistics.

On a similar day of reflection and action, International Women's Day in March 2011, Egyptian women, inspired by the recent political revolution in their country, gathered hopefully in Tahrir Square to declare their equal rights. Unfortunately many of these peaceful demonstrators were beaten and attacked. The attackers beat the women protestors because they didn't consider them representative of Egyptian women, but instead saw them as foreigners, activists, and liberals. In fact, the majority of the women protesting that day were Egyptian by birth and Muslim.

The level of harassment that Egyptian women live under is hard to imagine for those of us who live in relatively egalitarian societies. Cairo, in particular, is thought to be one of the worst cities in the world for women in terms of the prevalence and ferocity of sexual harassment.

In a recent study by **The Egyptian Center for Women's Rights**, a staggering 83% of Egyptian women said they'd been sexually harassed and about half of them reported abuse on a daily basis. Of these victims of harassment, more than 72% were veiled. In this same study, 62% of Egyptian men admitted to harassing women, with 53% of the men blaming women for "bringing it on themselves."

I've visited Egypt twice, once before the Arab Spring and once after, during my two-year journey. During the second visit, I experienced a heighted level of physical and verbal aggression. For instance, while standing on the side of the road trying to hail a taxi, cars would purposely veer toward me so I'd have to jump back out of the way to avoid being hit.

During this same visit, my Egyptian friend Inji and I were driving home after visiting a jazz club. A group of men in another car pulled dangerously close alongside us, making lewd gestures, and repeatedly cutting us off. I asked Inji why we didn't just drive to the police station for help. She told me that the police would simply laugh at us.

When we walked along the streets together, Inji would repeatedly turn around and scream at the men who were insulting us by making lewd comments about our bodies. It was not uncommon that men would follow us, stand uncomfortably close, and touch us inappropriately.

The impact of this unrelenting harassment on Egyptian women's self-esteem is profound, causing women to adapt their behavior to live in an increasingly hostile society. Inji has written a revealing report detailing how sexual harassment is increasing the carbon footprint of Egyptian women. Since it's dangerous for women to walk, bicycle, ride the subway (even in women-only cars), and ride alone in taxis, the only alternative is to drive by car.

After just one short week, I even found myself modifying my behavior. While walking down the crowded streets of Cairo, I would walk without making eye contact, especially with men. Usually an open, outgoing person, I began to look at the ground or to stare straight ahead to avoid any sort of engagement. Another girl, a visiting Norwegian, said she would no longer smile, making her public face a frown to discourage unwanted advances. How are we women supposed to go out and conquer the world when we can't even pick up our heads?

Outrage at this sort of constant sexual aggression led Rebecca Chiao to develop *HarassMap,* a Cairo-centered tech tool that seeks to end the social acceptability of sexual harassment. Basically, the tool enables women to use their mobile phones to report an incidence of sexual harassment via SMS messaging as soon as it happens.

HarassMap then maps these anonymous reports online, so that women can see and avoid high-risk areas of the city. By amassing the real-time data of these incidents, the texts provide valuable evidence of the volume of sexual harassment on the streets.

Women can subscribe to HarassMap for free and receive a text alert when a report has been filed within 10-12 miles (20 km) of their location. The program also refers women who have been attacked to legal aid, psychological counseling, and other health services.

While HarassMap is a great idea, the effectiveness of the program is weakened by the sheer number of attacks. Ironically, the reason some women are not fully utilizing HarassMap is because they don't have time during the day to report all the abuse they receive. My feeling about this: red hot anger!

South Africa is another country where women deal with a frightening amount of physical violence. This is one of the most crime-ridden societies in the world, with a murder rate that's eight times higher than in the United States.

South Africa also leads the world in the number of rapes against women. Here's an ugly snapshot of this country's gender violence:

- 1,300 women are raped in South Africa every day.
- A woman is raped in South Africa every 27 seconds.
- It is estimated that 1 in 2 South African women will be raped.
- A woman born in South Africa has a greater chance of being raped than learning how to read.

What enrages me most is the attitude underlying these figures. Of South African men interviewed, 37% admit to committing rape. In addition almost 7% admit to participating in a gang rape or "jackrolling." Furthermore, two-thirds of South African rapists say they have a sense of sexual entitlement during the rape. Others state their reasons for rape include a desire to punish women who rejected or angered them. Perhaps most chilling were rapists who said they raped "out of boredom."

The 2010 study which provided many of these appalling statistics also questioned South African men who said they knew somebody who had been raped. A full 16% believed that the rape survivor had enjoyed the experience and had asked for it. In another study, one-third of South African rapists said they didn't feel guilty about committing rape. South Africa has now created a culture of rampant rapism.

And while there isn't a whole lot of good to say about this story, there is perhaps the slightest of silver linings—South Africans are beginning to protest. In 2012, *SlutWalks* took place in Johannesburg and Cape Town, where more than 2,000 marchers showed up.

During a SlutWalk, participants protest against the explaining or excusing of rape by referring to any aspect of a woman's appearance. The global protests started in April 2011, when a Toronto Police officer suggested that "women should avoid dressing like sluts in order not to be victimized."

SlutWalks, which take place all over the world, aren't encouraging the idea that women wear provocative clothing or sexual promiscuity. Instead marchers are rejecting the attitude that somehow rape victims themselves are to blame, that they asked to be raped because of what they wear or how they act.

Women attend the marches dressed how they like, some provocatively to drive home the point, but many in everyday clothing. During a South African march, at least one woman marched in the outfit that she was wearing when she was raped.

I have to admit, I'm not sure how South African women function in a society where rape is an everyday occurrence. I was uneasy most of my time in South Africa, where dishing out the details of the latest violent crime is typical dinner table conversation. I can't tell you how many horror stories were nonchalantly shared—not by travelers—but by resident South Africans themselves.

People often ask me what I think of South Africa. My answer: I have a love / hate relationship with it. It has a physical beauty that is astounding and I've made some fabulous friends there. But there is an ugliness that runs deep, the product of decades of inequality and inhumanity that is still festering.

Men, who are physically stronger, are taking it out on women, who are now victimized twice over. Once by the ravages of apartheid that still linger and again at the hands of the men who continue to feel powerless in an unjust society. If the state of constantly brutalized women in Egypt and South Africa doesn't fuel our anger, what will?

Crazy Kim – Nha Trang, Vietnam

The way children are treated gives us great insight into a society. I become outraged upon hearing of children being traded, given away, or sold in many parts of the world. The thought of their little bodies broken and discarded at the hands of adults is particularly nauseating.

Growing up around Pacific Island cultures, it never ceased to surprise me that Marshallese parents (named after the island nation called the Marshall Islands, part of the Federated States of Micronesia) routinely give away their children if a neighbor or relative asks for them. Or if a child is no longer wanted, they are simply given to another. Or in Samoan culture where children are encouraged not to cry and are even mocked if they show signs of distress.

In Southeast Asia, it's not uncommon for children—and their bodies—to be seen as commodities. This crassness struck me most while watching a *Muay Thai* match in southern Thailand. Thailand's national sport is characterized by eight points of contact, where boxers use their hands, feet, elbows, and knees to land blows against their opponent. So when I went to the ring, I was expecting there to be some violence and blood and brutality.

At first I equated Thailand's version of all-contact kick-boxing with bull fighting and wasn't going to go to see the spectacle. But then I rationalized that, unlike the bull, the fighters in Muay Thai didn't die in the end. I also believed that it was an adult who made the decision to get in the ring to fight. I was wrong on this last account.

I didn't expect that children would participate and be seriously injured during fights. Of the nine bouts I saw that night, four featured kids, some as young as seven-years old. I found the children's participation hateful since the children wore no safety gear or head protection. In one of the early fights, one of the youngest children was knocked unconscious, most likely suffering a concussion. Adding to my utter dismay was seeing the children's mothers in their corners screaming for them to fight harder. Appalling.

At the end of each bout, the children were paid 200 baht, the equivalent of $6, for taking their beating in the ring. I watched how parents eagerly waited in the corners, not to comfort their kids, but to snatch the dirty bills out of the hands of their blurry-eyed and bleeding youngsters.

I was astonished, unable to believe that parents would send their young children out to fight, let alone with no protective gear. But apparently, I was the only one who felt this way. All around me the crowd was wild during the matches, with bets being placed on the child most likely to be victorious.

And it wasn't just local Thais enjoying the sport. A French tourist sitting next to me had brought his six-year old daughter, who was obviously traumatized to see her fellow first-graders being pulverized. I asked him why he had come and he admitted that, like me, he didn't realize that it would be so violent. Nevertheless, he and his cringing daughter, hands over her eyes during most of the matches, stayed until the bitter end.

After my initial shock and some fierce internal deliberation, I decided not to leave, even though I found the whole experience abominable. Instead I chose to stay and document what I saw. I thought by photographing and videoing the brutality I could perhaps draw more attention to what I consider an inhuman and blatant disregard for children's safety.

At the very least, I would like there to be laws to protect children while fighting in the ring. In the UK, where children also participate in Muay Thai tournaments, there are rules to protect the kids. For instance, head shots are illegal in children's fights and full padding is required. This is certainly a start.

The deeper issue, however, is why families agree to have one of their young sons risk serious bodily injury—especially brain trauma— for the sake of $6. Sadly, the answer is obvious. It's the money. In the developing world, where there is entrenched poverty and need, some children are seen as a way to make money. We just have to skip over to the neighboring countries of Cambodia and Vietnam to see more children being used. And I mean literally used.

Most of the time while I was traveling throughout Southeast Asia, I stayed in small guest houses and hotels. Not the hostels filled with backpackers and not international hotel chains, but small, three-star hotels in the heart of capital cities.

Each morning, I would get up and head down to the dining room to avail myself of the free breakfast. It was there, in the bright sun of a new day, that the harsh light of reality was most clear. Surrounding me would be tables of three of four individuals, usually a middle-aged Caucasian or Asian man, and two or three young (sometimes very young) Cambodian girls. I stared daggers at the men, trying to convey my utter disgust at their wanton actions.

While I sullenly drank my tea, these girls, with their long, wet hair, and their skimpy clothes would be shoveling food in their mouths at an astounding rate. There was no conversation at the table. And the men nearly always looked ashamed, eyes downcast. I'd like to think they too were appalled at the tender age of the girls, so apparent in full daylight. But this may be hoping for too much, as the same transaction would occur later that night, night after night. One man, two or three girls in one bedroom, followed by an early morning shower and hearty breakfast for the child prostitutes.

While the exact number of child prostitutes is unknown, child trafficking and the sexual exploitation of children is an entrenched economic reality. It's estimated that this global criminal enterprise traffics at least one million children every year. Of these trafficked victims, 98% are female and 95% experience sexual or physical violence.

End Child Prostitution & Trafficking (ECPAT) brings together a global network of organizations and individuals who are working to end child prostitution, child pornography, and the trafficking of children for sexual purposes. Many years ago, I volunteered for the U.S. arm of this organization, which seeks to protect children who are sexually exploited by Americans who travel abroad. A full 25% of sex tourists—child predators and pedophiles—are American and Canadian men who are traveling overseas to buy children for sex.

I spent several months working with the founder and her team, helping them to form a strategy to engage corporations within the travel industry, such as hotel chains, airlines, and tour agencies— those on the frontline of child trafficking. We sought to provide them with tools to help stop child exploitation. Not only did I volunteer with them for many months, but I also happily gave multiple donations to support their important work.

While supporting organizations working to engage key players is a crucial part of preventing child exploitation, I also like to provide direct support to help girls who have already been victimized. During my travels and with the input of my readers, the GoErinGo! Fund made a $250 donation to an organization called *Hagar Cambodia,* which provides therapy and aftercare for girls who have been subjected to sex trafficking, sexual abuse, and exploitation in Cambodia.

Another nonprofit working on behalf of Cambodia girls is an organization called *Lotus Petals*, which purchases bikes and repairs kits for girls living in the countryside. By providing heavy-terrain bicycles to hundreds of at-risk and exploited girls, this group is helping to keep girls in school and to end the cycle of poverty in the country.

An organization called the *ChildSafe Network* also works to solve trafficking through economic investment programs and greater awareness. ChildSafe seeks to protect Cambodian children by promoting a ChildSafe logo, that allows tourists to instantly recognize business establishments, including restaurants, bars, hotels, tour agencies, and tuk tuk drivers, that refuse to tolerate child prostitution on their premises.

If I had known to look for the ChildSafe logo, I would have definitely changed my Southeast Asian hotel booking habits to ensure that I would not give my tourist dollars to businesses that turn a blind eye to child sexual exploitation. Finding the ChildSafe organization on my last day in Phnom Penh, I eagerly went in to learn more about their good work and purchase several ChildSafe products, including a pretty cool pair of black karate pants. These products are made by parents, providing them with an income that allows their children to stay in school.

Another type of child exploitation in Southeast Asia that is unfortunately gaining in popularity is orphan tourism. This unsettling trend was brought to my attention by my Twitter friend Shawn, who pointed out that many nonprofit organizations are not being run in a child-centric way. (To put it mildly.)

Orphan tourism is shorthand for nonprofits that cater to tourists that seek to volunteer at the expense of properly helping those in need. This trend is particularly evident in orphanages in developing countries, where neglectful volunteering practices more often occur. These organizations lack safety procedures, such as background checks. Requiring long-term commitments from volunteers can also help protect children who are already vulnerable, as can prohibitions on filming and photographing children.

As I learned about the extent of orphan tourism in Southeast, I decided to forgo a stint volunteering in a Cambodian orphanage, one of the engagements in which I was most looking forward. Instead I sought out non-intrusive volunteer opportunities, such as environmental conservation and community development work, which satisfied my yearning to learn more about Cambodian culture and society, and yet protected the fragile children who had already suffered enough.

I found one of these volunteer gigs in the central Vietnamese city of Nha Trang at a place called *Crazy Kim's*, which sounds like a bar. Hey wait, it is a bar. But it's also a school for teenagers and young adults during the daytime hours.

Proprietress Kimmy Le, a Canadian of Vietnamese origin, opened the school in 1996 to help educate Vietnamese street children. When she first started Kim bribed the kids with a free lunch at the end of class each day, trading a meal for math and language tutoring.

Not only did the school teach language basics, it also taught children to be aware of sexual predators in this seaside resort town, where a mere $5,000 entitles pedophiles to "adopt" local Vietnamese children from poor families.

When Kimmy first opened her bar, she noted the presence of foreign pedophiles. Her response was to get beach children to wear T-shirts that said: "Child sex is a crime." She also has stickers on her bar that say "Child Sex Tourism: Don't turn away. Turn them in."

Unfortunately, child sexual exploitation hasn't ended in Vietnam. Instead, it has become more sophisticated and moved underground. Now run by criminal gangs, sex tourism is an integral part of the country's economic fabric. And unfortunately, most police aren't solving the problem, but profiting from it.

With street children and sex trafficking moving underground and out of sight, there is no longer a large population of street kids in need of free meals. So Kimmy changed her curriculum and now provides free English and computer classes to college-age students. Most of the pupils are studying for their TOEFL exam and some days as many as 120 attend her free school.

The morning I volunteered at Crazy Kim's, I got to sit in on three classes:

Robyn's class was studying how to reply to a job advertisement in the paper. Robyn is Australian and has been coming to Nha Trang to volunteer at Crazy Kim's for three months each summer for the last five years. That's dedication. The eight students in her advanced English class went through the want ad and were answering questions and discussing the qualifications necessary for the position. I served as a mock interviewer for the students.

Mr. Hien's class was writing essays. This large class of about twenty-five students were writing quietly for most of the time, except when they were giving cat calls and whooping it up when Mr. Hien and I took a picture together. Wish I could've read what they were writing.

Frank's class of twelve students downstairs was practicing speaking with a twenty-year old volunteer from Sweden named Sophia. They were talking a lot about what makes Sweden unique and then switched to a conversation about Vietnam's attributes. The students, several of which were studying to be nurses and accountants, all sat at the edge of a beer-stained pool table which served as a communal desk.

What I like about Crazy Kim's operation is that Kimmy has found a way to engage foreigners as volunteers that is safe for the youngsters she serves. Tourists share their native English and their knowledge of foreign business practices. And the beneficiaries, the college students, are old enough not be victimized by ill-meaning tourists.

Still I feel almost uncontrollable anger when I think of all the children forced into prostitution and the adults preying on the vulnerable. Child brutality in any form is repulsive, as is beating and sexually harassing women. What I've learned over the years is to not just give mean glares, but to take action. In the future, when confronted with obvious abuse, I'll heed Kimmy's wise advice: "Don't turn away, turn them in."

Chapter 7: **SURPRISE**

Most of the time I love being surprised. In fact, I consider it one of the best parts of traveling. Having no idea what's around the next corner is fabulously fun!

But not all surprises are amusing. During my two-year trek I had my fair share of the Good, the Bad and the Ugly, leaving in their wake a lasting impression—of wonder, disbelief and chagrin.

Tourist Tom – Antarctica

Antarctica was the region that surprised me the most on my travels. I thought my journey to the White Continent would be the trip of a lifetime and so I decided to splurge and lay out about $4,000 for the 10-day trip. In my mind, it was the grand finale to two years of constant travel. I thought: "Just this once, because you'll never be back." Wrong!

I loved the Antarctic so much there's no question in my mind that I'll return. That's how truly fabulous and fascinating the continent is. There is nowhere else like it in the world—offering an amazing discovery every single day. Antarctica is addictive.

The guy who convinced me to travel to the southern tip of the world was Tourist Tom, an Australian school teacher who won his money to travel around the world by playing the Down Under version of *Deal or No Deal*. True story.

I met Tom while sailing from Cartagena, Colombia to Panama City, via the beautiful San Blas islands. During the days at sea on a small sailboat, he entertained us by whipping out his computer and playing the game show episode that got him his plane ticket. His photos and videos of the White Continent were so compelling (especially the up-close footage of his naked polar plunge), that I changed my travel plans. In the end, I hustled through Bolivia, bypassed Paraguay, whizzed through Argentina's Iguazú Falls to make it to the southern-most city in the world: Ushuaia.

As luck would have it, I was trolling a travel web site trying to find out how I could nab an eleventh-hour sailing, when I spotted a query from two Americans, Dawn and Josh, looking for a third person to share their triple cabin. I instantly replied and a few days later I was sending in my deposit to secure my spot on the first expedition ship out for the 2012 Antarctic season. Score!

Since I was a last-minute sign up, the ship's sea kayaking adventure (which I would have dearly loved) was all booked up, but I still got to ice camp on the continent—a rare treat! Our campsite was in Neko Harbor, on the Danco Coast.

Neko Harbor is simply stunning. For one thing, it contains a massive glacier that calves continually. Calving occurs when large (as in sky-scraper sized) chunks of ice fall off a glacier or iceberg. This is accompanied by a monstrous thunder-like cracking followed by an enormous ice block splintering from the main ice shelf and falling into the water, creating a 20 foot (6 m) high splash. It's quite dramatic.

So I couldn't help but open the tent door all night long to watch. See, the falling ice chunks create small waves that lap onto shore and the bigger pieces were creating small tsunamis that were threatening our camp site.

This was slightly worrying since a few years back a wave created by calving ice roared onto shore and sucked twelve campers back into the icy water. I think that would be a rude awakening. Since my tent mate and I had decided to pitch our tent beachside, with the best possible view of the glacier, I was on tsunami alert. I spent the entire night zipping and unzipping the tent flap each time I heard a loud splintering of ice, followed by an extra-large splash. It was a cold long night, as my tent mate repeatedly told me.

In addition to the tsunami watch, I was also paying particular attention to the toilet. The camp toilet was al fresco in the extreme, just a plastic commode surrounded by an ice wall to shield your privates from prying eyes.

Disrobing from multiple parkas and exposing your back side to the frigid cold is a semi-shocking experience and not one you want to have to repeatedly endure—especially when you need to crawl out of a warm sleeping bag to brave the cold air on your butt. To ward against this unpleasant experience, I discovered the #1 rule of ice camping: Reduce all fluid intake.

What with the midnight sun shining, an active glacier, and the brutal cold I continually let in with my manic zipping and un-zipping, we didn't get a lot of sleep that night. But who cares? We were ice camping on the mainland of Antarctica. An unforgettable experience!

Another highlight and complete surprise was the educational value of an Antarctic expedition. Each expedition ship is staffed with on-board naturalists and scientists providing insights on the native wildlife, the history of South Pole exploration, photography tips, and geology (my favorite!).

I learned so much about Antarctica that I didn't even know what I didn't know. Like Antarctica is:

- More than 5 million miles in size (larger than the U.S. and Mexico combined).
- Not really a concentrated land mass, but a series of islands that is covered by ice to form one large land (or ice) mass.
- 98% ice and comprises 70% of the world's fresh water.
- The driest, highest, windiest, and coldest of all the continents. (Actually I might have guessed this one.)
- Claimed by seven countries: Australia, Argentina, Chile, New Zealand, Norway, France, and the UK.

Also new and surprising to me was the amount of wildlife in Antarctica. As the coldest, darkest place on Earth, I had mistakenly assumed there would not be a whole lot of animals about. But there were, especially penguins. It's amazing how long you'll sit perfectly still in the snow to watch these funny birds waddle past. On second thought, I might have been frozen in place.

Before my expedition, I thought all penguins were the same. But now I find myself watching programs like *Frozen Planet* on TV and showing off my new-found knowledge of these flightless birds. For instance, Gentoo penguins are the fastest underwater swimmers, reaching speeds more than 20 miles (36 km) per hour.

Adélie penguins are named after the wife of French explorer Jules Dumont d'Urville (how romantically French). Adélie penguins live in the sea except when they come ashore to build their nests and breed. Climate change and the reduction of ice has hit the Adélie population hard, decreasing it by 65% in the last 25 years.

Chinstrap penguins are my favorite; so cute, with a thin black line outlining their faces and holding on their black helmets of hair, I mean, feathers. Fortunately, they have healthy colonies of more than twelve million. Chinstraps can live up to twenty years and are considered the most aggressive of our finned friends.

And finally Macaroni penguins are the ones with the distinctive yellow-feather crown. Their breeding colonies can be up to 100,000 thick and they only spend 3-4 weeks nesting on land before returning to the ocean. Since we were there during mating season, we saw a lot of this nesting activity. Penguin love abounds.

Our expedition also saw three kinds of seals. Did you know that seals don't have ears, but they can still hear? Startling. And seals' noses automatically close in the water and can stay pinched shut for up to thirty minutes? Weird. Learning these types of fascinating facts are what make Antarctic adventures so entertaining.

We also had a few great sightings of whales from our ship, including Orcas with a baby in tow. Part of the dolphin family, there are about 25,000 Orcas plying the Antarctic waters. Humpback whales also made an appearance. We spied one gliding right by our porthole window, fin vertical in the air, saluting us as it swam past.

If you are an animal lover, Antarctica is the place for you. Really really love animals? You can even volunteer on the continent. This volunteer stint has you sitting on the ice all day...wait for it...penguin counting.

Doug, one of the staff on my expedition ship, got his start working in Antarctica by volunteering. He was desperate to find any job, even an unpaid one, which would allow him to explore the Antarctic region. In exchange for a plush berth aboard a National Geographic expedition ship, he signed up to help the **National Science Foundation** (NSF) conduct research studying the effects of increased tourism on Antarctica's flora and fauna. The initial study created a baseline from which physical and biological variables can be tracked over time.

Volunteers like Doug sit on the ice for six hours a day, recording the number of occupied penguin nests, the number of chicks per nest, and the age of chicks. They also monitored visitor impact by documenting footprints and walking paths, and tourist debris, such as cigarette butts, film canisters, and litter.

Surprisingly expedition tourism has been found to have increased penguin numbers, since tourists keep seals, penguins' main predator, away. Who would have thought that tourists tramping around on the ice would have a beneficial effect on Antarctic wildlife? This continent never ceases to amaze me. A surprise of the best kind, for sure.

Zorro – Romania to Bulgaria Road Trip

I got another oversized surprise when I met up with Zorro outside a bus station. My friend Brid and I had just arrived into the Romanian capital of Bucharest. Brid was in the station asking for directions to our hostel, while I waited outside with the luggage. That's when I spied Zorro, ankles casually crossed and leaning nonchalantly against his taxi. As intended, I was quite taken with the sight.

See, in all my travels, I find Romanian men to be the most handsome. As in tall, dark, and handsome. So I was a bit of a sitting duck when Zorro turned on his considerable charm. And Brid, being a good wing woman, only stoked the fires of lust.

Brid, an Irish gal, and I originally met in Ethiopia, where she and I and another Irish lassie named Paula, pooled resources to book a hiking excursion into the Simian Mountains. We had come to hike the hills and see the world-famous views. Unfortunately, the trip was a disaster. It rained the entire time with the mountains remained shrouded in a dense fog. One perk was that we got to see the glorious grass-eating baboons. It turned out to be mating season yet again and this time I was surrounded by baboon love. It was a messy affair.

The drab weather reminded Brid and Paula a little too much of the wet Irish countryside, so we separated and they went South in search of sun. Though we parted to travel our separate ways, Brid, Paula and I had become fast friends.

We kept in touch and Brid and I decided to meet up again, this time to explore Romania and Bulgaria. We fancied ourselves a good 'ole girls trip to the Black Sea. Brid was a great one to travel with, not only because she's Irish and friendly and all-around good fun, but also because she had been to Romania twice before.

Brid had visited a small village outside of Bucharest a few years earlier to volunteer. One night over a pint, Brid told me about her multiple trips volunteering overseas. First she went to Ecuador and then to Romania to work with emotionally disturbed children.

As a professional therapist, Brid specializes in play therapy, which helps children with severe behavioral problems express themselves through unstructured and non-directed play that can help diagnosis and heal their internal conflicts. During her overseas travels, Brid donates her time to children's homes, using her professional talents to help children, who would not normally be exposed to this type of advanced psychosocial training.

During her trips to Romania, Brid not only volunteered, but also made donations to the local orphanage where she was spending her time. Her volunteer engagement was arranged beforehand by a friend with ties to Romania and Brid had collected donations from family and friends before leaving Ireland.

During these volunteer stints, Brid learned a hard lesson: giving money away is not as easy as we all think. It's actually very difficult to give responsibly, ensuring that the organizations are honest and well run, and that the people and programs we're trying to help are the ones who benefit the most.

Brid originally planned to distribute the full $5,000 (£3,000) she had collected. Working in the children's home, she started talking to the staff to find out who should receive the funds. But the more questions she asked, the more confused she became. It was hard for her to determine who was needy and who was greedy. In the end, she only elected to donate about half the money, holding onto the remainder until she could return and better assess the situation.

During her second trip a year later, Brid traveled with her Romanian contact, a local who spoke the language and understood the Romanian culture. This local insight helped Brid discern which programs and people truly needed extra assistance and she donated the remainder of the funds. In the end, Brid felt good about her two-pronged giving strategy.

With two previous trips to Romania under her belt, Brid was in charge of navigating our adventure. That's my excuse for us being hustled on a joy ride almost all the way to Bulgaria. We were driven, of course by Zorro. (By the way, his real name was Doro, but we thought he said Zorro at first and it stuck. And he was working the swash-buckling swagger.)

We had intended to buy our bus tickets to Bulgaria as soon as we arrived. But it turns out there are no direct buses, so we needed to make several transfers to get to our ultimate destination: the Bulgarian beach town of Sozopol. We're talking at least 10-12 hours in a bus, losing mucho valuable beach time.

So Brid and I decided to go by train. It was in the cab on the way to the train station that we fell under the spell of Zorro. After a bit of small talk, we told him where we were trying to go. He magnanimously offered to drive us.

After a short negotiation and several phone calls on his end, we agreed on a price of $110 for door-to-door service from Bucharest to Sozopol, on the southern shore of the Black Sea, a total of 213 miles

(343 km). We were to leave at 9:00 am the next morning. He said the drive would take 5 hours.

At breakfast the next day, Brid and I chatted about our expectations. First, we knew Zorro would be driving a private car, not his taxi. We also speculated that he'd have a friend with him and their own luggage would be in the boot. We were right on all three accounts.

A 9:00 am sharp, Zorro pulled up in a small compact car with a buddy in the front seat. After reconfirming our deal and ensuring he could legally drive us across the border, the four of us set off on our road trip: Brid and I, Zorro and his buddy Flore.

It soon became apparent that neither of our escorts had ever been to Bulgaria before as they kept arguing with each other about the best route to take. Our only map was a page I had torn from my out-of-date travel book, which didn't have a whole lot of detail.

After an hour of noisy driving (they were arguing about how to get out of the city), we pulled into a gas station. They promptly asked us for half the fare so they could pay for petrol. From experience, Brid and I both knew this is standard procedure for long-range private transport in developing countries, so we forked over $55 and we were on our way.

Soon Zorro was perpetually holding out his hand for money—at the border for the car registration fee, for the road toll, to change currency from Romania Lei into Bulgarian Lev. By 11:00 am, we had already paid the full $110 fare.

Soon after crossing into Bulgaria, I asked to stop the car so I could get my stereo speakers out of my luggage. I wanted to listen to music on my iPod instead of boisterous Bulgarian radio. When I was digging around in the trunk, Flore, who was riding shotgun, showed me the bag they had brought along for the trip. It contained three bottles: one vodka and two whiskey. It was 11:30 a.m.

At 1:00 pm we pulled over and Zorro asked if we could buy him and Flore lunch. We actually didn't have enough money, since Brid and I had only exchanged enough Bulgarian Lev for us to eat. He grudgingly dipped into the fare to buy their own meals.

As we finished eating, Flore fetched the first bottle—the vodka. After a few quick shots, he confessed their plan to accompany us on our holiday. He suggested that we all drive to the beach, go to dinner and dancing, and they would stay the night. Surprise!

Brid and I were quick to set the record straight. Our first priority was to arrive safely in Sozopol, and then we could go out, but they would need to find their own place to stay. This news didn't go down so well.

Zorro then asked Brid if she would drive so he could drink with Flore. He seemed to forget that we were paying him to drive. So we reminded him of our deal, stressing that (obviously) he couldn't drink since he was behind the wheel. After more than six hours in the car, it was turning into a long afternoon.

Ten hours later, we finally pulled into Sozopol and made our way to the hotel Brid and I had booked ahead of time. We went to our room to get cleaned up and set up a time to meet up with them later that night. When we came out of the hotel, they were sitting in the car where we had left them, holding tightly onto their hopes and what little remained of the two bottles of whiskey.

Before setting out for the night, Brid and I had agreed that we would go to dinner and that we would pay for it. Even though they had been hitting us up all day for extra cash, we felt slightly bad that they had completely underestimated the cost of the drive down and they would be eating a big chunk of it. Besides, we had saved oodles of money by not taking the bus or the train.

So we decided to offer them dinner as a thank you for driving us down, making it clear that after dinner we would go our own way. Zorro found our offer insulting and refused the invitation flat. Flore, who had very little English, just sat, looking totally confused by the whole exchange. After our dinner invitation was declined, we said goodbye and walked away.

Zorro trailed us few minutes later in the car, rolling up behind us as we walked down the hill toward the seaside restaurants. He wanted to explain that he didn't take the job of driving us to Bulgaria for the money, but for the "joy of the trip" with us. Batting his long lashes, he confessed that they didn't have enough money to return home.

He made one more last-ditch effort to persuade us to fill the gas tank, give them a place to stay, or at least give them enough money so they could call their mother to wire them extra funds. No, no, and no. Apparently Zorro and Flore were two grown men without a penny to their names.

Now it was our turn to be insulted and after a few choice words, Brid and I again walked away and this time didn't look back. That night, we went out, had a great dinner of fresh fish and a few cocktails. We ended up staying nearly a week, lounging on the beach, reading trashy novels, buying our food from the boys at the beach huts, and exploring the holiday hotspot that is Sozopol.

In the end, Zorro and Flore spent the night sleeping in their car, supremely shocked that we could resist their charms and their bad intentions.

Brenda – Darwin, Australia

I was pleasantly surprised by the far more wholesome charm I found during my last stop on the Australian continent. After six weeks of touring, I was in the Northern Territories metropolis of Darwin. I went there to volunteer with a fabulous organization: ***Darwin Community Arts*** (DCA). DCA is an incubator for social enterprises and nonprofits, promoting the arts and community development within the city.

One of my favorite DCA program is called *My Sister's Kitchen*, founded by my friend Brenda. The program brings together refugee women to swap recipes and share stories. By providing a friendly, neutral space, refugee women from different countries come together in a communal kitchen to tell of their experiences in their home countries and their new life in Australia. Lots of dishing all the way around.

I was lucky to be working with DCA on the day they were hosting their monthly community dinner. I joined the women of My Sister's Kitchen about 10:00 am, taking my position beside a dedicated group of ladies from Burma to wash, chop, and shred vegetables for that night's meal. The menu offered a multi-ethnic mix, including an egg curry, a traditional slaw, and all-important rice.

Our special guests that evening were a group of teenage girls from the Tiwi Islands, located about 50 miles (80 km) off Australia's northern coast. This was the first time I had even heard of the islands, which rose from the sea 7,000 years ago and are home to just 2,500 people. The islanders have purposely kept their paradise isolated from the rest of Australia. Visits by outsiders to the islands are restricted, so having a group of Tiwi Islanders was indeed an honor.

In addition to our communal dinner, the evening's festivities featured several musical performances. First we watched an energetic dance quartet performed by refugees from the Democratic Republic of the Congo, accompanied by taped music from their homeland. Then came Australian children and teens of Irish-Australian descent, proudly demonstrating their high-kicking Celtic dancing.

It was the incongruity of these two completely opposite forms of dance that really showcased the charm of the evening and underscored the diversity of Darwin's population. That, plus the fact that the Celtic dancers were joined in high-stepping fashion by one of the Congolese men during their finale. The man's Lord of the Dance parody, while a tad disrespectful, was hilariously funny.

Rounding out the evening's entertainment was a dancer from Nepal, a Burmese singer, and a demonstration by an electronic band that fascinated the children with its computer-driven techno-music. Quite the eclectic collection. Which, of course, is exactly the point of My Sister's Kitchen: to bring together Darwin residents of all backgrounds to celebrate the community's ethnic and cultural range. I admit, it was an enchanting evening, full of surprise and delight.

After such an endearing time, I wasn't quite prepared for the surprise of my next adventure. My next stop after Australia was a sailing expedition to Indonesia's Nusa Tengara island chain. This was my third trip to Indonesia and I specifically booked this passage so I could see the Komodo dragons in their natural habitat.

I originally heard about Komodo dragons while living in Hong Kong in the early 1990s. My neighbor John had visited and come back with great tales of these blood-thirsty beasts! He showed me a blurry photo of a Komodo dragon racing inches from his foot as it went to tear apart a tethered goat. That's all it took—the image of these salivating pre-historic beasts was lodged in my brain and I decided back then that I had to see them in person.

Twenty years ago, you could pay an extra fee and witness a live goat being torn apart by dozens of frenzied dragons. Now the Komodo experience is run by national park rangers and is more humane, which means no more animal sacrifices for tourists.

Despite the banned bloodletting, seeing the Komodos is a rare treat. There are only about 2,500 dragons left, all them living on the 3 islands that make up Komodo National Park: Komodo, Rinca, and Padar. The boat tour I signed up for took me to two of these islands.

My foray to see the dragons on Rinca was best. The tour was led by a very patient guide who actually helped us spot dragons hiding in their natural habitat. Since our group was small, it was easy to be quiet and spot these elusive creatures. During our walking tour, we saw at least six dragons in the wild: head up, alert in the tall grass; sunning themselves flat on rocky outcrops; slithering along the ground. I was exhilarated to see them up close—I was practically in Jurassic Park!

We ended up hiking twice as long as the allotted time, the whole group enthused with seeing more and more dragons. During the hike, the only thing keeping us from being dinner was a forked stick. When one of the rascals got too close, the rangers would use the forked end to hold down the dragon's neck and use the pointed end to pop it in the nose. I have to admit, those beasts moved surprisingly quick for their size and that stick came in handy a few times.

Although Komodo dragons are deadly, their jaws aren't strong enough to kill large prey. Instead they lunge at their main diet, let's say a water buffalo or deer, and bite them in a soft area like the belly. It's the dragon's saliva that is poisonous and slowly kills the animal. When it's dead, or nearly, the dragons come to finish them off. This whole stalking process can take up to three weeks, with the dragons patiently following their prey until they finally succumb to the venomous spit.

Being a Komodo dragon ranger can be a dangerous job. One ranger was climbing down the ladder going to the outhouse one night when a dragon bit him on the ankle. Another man was attacked in his office and was bitten several times before his fellow rangers could rescue him.

The last person to actually die from a Komodo attack was a small child about twenty years ago. The child's mother had thoughtlessly thrown some food scraps out the window. The dragon, lured by the smell of the food, was hiding under the house, which was on stilts to keep the dragons at bay. When the innocent child came out to play, it pounced. The child bled to death before help could arrive.

Although an antidote exists that will counteract the Komodo's toxic saliva, there are only limited stores, and these are located on Bali, a full two-day boat ride away from Komodo National Park. I find it strange they don't even store a small amount at the National Park itself, which, as I mentioned, is the only place where the dragons live.

To my surprise, my real fear in Indonesia came, not from my close-up encounter with these deadly beasts, but from the five-day boat ride that took me there. During our sail, our small boat encountered several significant storms during the first days of our voyage. You may be asking: "How bad could the stormy weather have been?" Pretty bad. Especially on a rickety boat, crewed by teenagers sailing in shark-infested waters. A number of German girls were heard praying loudly at night.

If you travel in Southeast Asia, you're bound to hear stories about wooden boats sinking, usually due to overcrowding and rotting wood. It's actually pretty scary stuff and occurs with appalling regularity. I was hoping that we wouldn't become one of the statistics.

In an effort to make the voyage more tolerable, most of us travelers paid an extra $100 for a cabin room. The rest slept on the deck. The two options for the deck-dwellers were to sleep out in the elements or under the cover of the common room, where smoking was permitted. Tough choice for them: nightly asphyxiation or near drowning when the waves started breaking over the deck rail the second night at sea.

You'd think "deck class" would be the inferior sleeping accommodation. But no. Worse than sleeping in the rain and wind and choking on smoke was travelling "cabin class." I was given a shared cabin, with a stacked berth, ironically the size of a casket. I wasn't amused.

My roommate was an intrepid 63-year-old Dutch woman. She and I tried desperately to prop the cabin door open for some air and sanity.

We tried for hours, using shoes, back packs, and water bottles, but the rocking of the boat was too heavy and with each swell the door banged shut. It was like a sledgehammer hitting next to your head every thirty seconds. There was no choice. The cabin door would not only need to be closed, but also locked, to keep it from mercilessly slamming all night. A heart-thumping decision.

That first night, as I lay in my coffin-sized bunk, I rehearsed in my head my exact movements in case I thought the boat was going down. Over and over I imagined lunging at the lock and whipping the door open, before throwing myself on the deck—hopefully to be washed overboard where I could try to swim in the dark to safety. This was my Grand Escape Plan.

The rocking became so drastic that several women tied themselves to their beds with sarongs to keep from falling out during the night. They were in the inside berths and I didn't want to scare them with my Grand Escape Plan idea, especially since in their scenario they would have the extra step of untying a wet knot while under water. Gulp.

But wait a minute. What's the likelihood of a fully loaded Indonesian boat going down in a storm in the Indian Ocean? Precisely. Nobody slept wink. But while all twenty-six of us passengers were a little concerned about the sea-worthiness of our vessel, I had an extra surprise in store.

My cabin mate unfortunately fell in the bathroom on the first day. Her mishap was regrettable, but not entirely unexpected. The three bathrooms were a combo toilet / shower, so you were standing in several inches or more of water and soap suds and urine each time you entered the stall. Couple this with the fierce rocking of the boat and very few lights to guide your way down the exposed slippery steps, and a nasty fall was almost pre-ordained.

Since my cabin mate (her name is withheld for reasons that will soon become apparent), almost broke her neck in the slimy bathroom stall, she didn't want to venture downstairs to the toilet at night. Her solution was my nightmare.

She asked the cabin boy to station a bucket outside our cabin so she could simply use it as a chamber pot at night instead of risking her death on the wet stairs. No less than five times during the night she would slam the coffin door open, step outside, and sit on the bucket. Naked.

That's right, while I was rehearsing my Grand Escape Plan, I'd look over and see her there sitting on a 10-gallon plastic bucket, boobs resting on knees, in the moonlight. I got depressed thinking that this could be my last sight on earth.

At the half-way point, with still one more Komodo island to visit, more than eighteen people jumped ship. Now, some of you might be wondering why I too didn't leave this scary sailing scenario, but we I had come to see dragons and Komodo dragons I would see! I stuck it out for the full five days.

With all the extra bunk space, I requested an upgrade to a cabin of my own. Luckily, I made good friends with our Cruise Director Nardin, (honestly I think my knowledge of John Denver lyrics helped) and he gave me my own space. I actually think the crew felt a little sorry for me since everyone on the boat knew about the bare-assed bucket situation. I mean, the crew were the ones who had to empty the bucket in the morning. Or at least half of it. The other half of the urine / throw-up mix had sloshed onto the deck outside our cabin door by morning. So gross.

So an upgrade! I was thrilled with my new luxurious cabin that allowed me an extra foot of headroom and no hazardous waste. I was so pleased I didn't even care about the bed bugs biting my neck from the filthy pillows.

Looking back, the thing that freaks me out the most? I actually thought this Komodo dragon safari was one of the best adventures of my trip. Even in the stormy dead of night, with visions of a shipwreck keeping me awake, and smells of urine and puke punctuating the heavy air, I was reveling in what can only be described as an extremely ugly situation.

Indonesian ugliness meets pristine Antarctic goodness mixed with the badness of Romanian rogues. Ah, travel. A surprise under every iceberg, hidden in an island's tall grass, and tucked away deep inside the car boot. But that's part of the reason why we go. The lure of the unknown and the knowledge that surprises are lurking just beyond our imagination. Travel is too tantalizing to resist.

Chapter 8: **PAIN**

When I think of pain, I don't mean physical pain, but the pain we inflict on one another, the needless pain caused through wanton ruin—of people, of our environment, of endangered animals. I'm not talking about injury or illness, but unnecessary suffering caused by cruelty and greed.

All too often I saw evidence of pain and suffering during my travels, witnessing the despair of an entire country, the decimation of pristine habitats, and the harming of precious children through sinister actions. These memories of deliberate destruction are the definition of pain for me. These are the images that both hurt and haunt me.

Pol Pot – The Killings Fields, Cambodia

Of the 388 Killing Fields sites throughout Cambodia, I visited just one, a Buddhist memorial in the village of Choeung Ek, outside the capital of Phnom Penh. In Choeung Ek alone, there are 129 mass graves, with an estimated 20,000 people killed in the surrounding fields. The largest known grave contained 450 bodies. Another nearby grave was the burial site of more than 100 women and children. Next to that grave was a tall tree, nicknamed "The Killing Tree," where babies were killed by smashing their skulls against the trunk and then tossed into an open pit. This is a place of true and unimaginable horror.

The Cambodia genocide that occurred between 1975 and1978 was remarkable for many gruesome reasons, but especially because it was the first ever genocide of a people against their own kind, with no distinction of race, ethnicity, or religion.

Cambodia's conflict was purely a class war and the result of one mad man: Pol Pot, who promoted a brutal type of agrarian socialism that relegated the country's educated urban class to the countryside to work on collective farms. During Pol Pot's four-year reign, his policies ended the lives of nearly a quarter of the country's population.

It was my second morning in Phnom Penh. I flagged a tuk tuk to take me out to Choeung Ek, where I hired a local graduate student and guide named Ouch to take me through the memorial. Ouch was an excellent teacher, patiently answering my uninformed questions, such as "How could the Khmer Rouge kill all of the educated people in such a short time?"

Ouch explained how the Khmer Rouge, after taking Phnom Penh, announced that the capital would be bombed in a number of hours, forcing everyone to evacuate. The sudden relocation was calculating, separating people from the support systems of family and friends. Entire neighborhoods were divided and displaced to far-off provinces.

Pol Pot's policies not only isolated the professional class, but also sought to physically and emotionally weaken them through a campaign of forced manual labor. He also abolished the monetary system so no one could buy food. As a result, access to food was rationed by the government and given to the peasants first, letting the educated people go hungry.

The largest emotional trauma occurred when the Khmer Rouge separated parents from their children. The government then started inducting the children into their "Year Zero" ideology, which mandated that the existing culture and traditions must be completely destroyed before a new revolutionary order could take hold. These policies pitted children against parents in Cambodia's new order, effectively breaking the backbone of the country's culture of *filial piety, the* centuries-old tradition of respecting one's parents and ancestors.

The regime also killed families en mass. Many innocent children were murdered because the Khmer Rouge believed that "to cut the grass, you must remove the roots"—meaning that if there was a traitor, every member of the traitor's family needed to be eliminated.

Worse yet, many of the deaths were unimaginably brutal since the army was trying to save ammunition. As a result, executions were carried out with everyday objects, such as umbrellas or walking sticks, or farm tools, like hoes and machetes. Once used as instruments of death, you'll never quite look at these mundane objects quite the same again.

A Buddhist stupa with seventeen tiers stands in the center of Choeung Ek. Each tier houses a different type of bone: skulls, femurs, jaw bones. It gave me pause to look up at the tower of bleached bones, seeing them all jumbled together in a glass case.

As nauseating as this image was, the vision that haunts me the most was what emerged from the muddy fields. The night before my visit there was a heavy rainfall, and with more than 9,000 bodies yet to be exhumed, bones had started to come up through the earth. So as you walk on the dirt paths surrounding the memorial, you actually need to step over large bones protruding from the ground and bits of faded clothing half buried. It was shocking and still gives me shivers.

Not only did the Khmer Rouge army kill out in the fields, but also in the abandoned schools (Year Zero had no need for education), which were used as torture chambers. The principal prison was a former high school called S-21, now officially called the *Toul Sleng Genocide Museum*. The prison was known for its barbaric acts of torture, where methods such as water boarding were routinely used.

While walking through the bare-boned museum, I systematically went through every room to look at the photographed faces of the victims of torture, abuse, and experimentation. The viewing was difficult to see. By the fourth room, I was wondering how many more there were. Answer: more than twenty. Adjacent to the photographs of the victims, hung black and white images of the teenage guards who did most of the killing. Their faces were so very, very young.

Despite being depressed by the sight of such profane destruction, I spent an entire day at the Killing Fields and S-21. When I travel, I go to these types of memorials because I feel it's necessary to truly understand a country, its culture, and its people. To ignore or remain willfully ignorant of such an integral part of Cambodia's past is to ignore the crimes that have been committed.

I also believe that by looking at the victims' faces, I can bear witness to the suffering endured by these innocent people. After they had braved so much pain, the least I could do was be there to acknowledge their sacrifice. And in this small way, I hope to help ensure that their suffering isn't completely forgotten.

A further pain inflicted on Cambodians by Pol Pot and his regime is still evident in the land mines he and his youth army planted. This is a pain Cambodia shares with its neighbor Laos.

America's "secret" war against Laos in the late 1960s and early 1970s is still causing unimaginable harm, with a plethora of unexploded devices, referred to as UXOs, left behind to torment the Lao people.

The entire country has inherited the terrible legacy as being the world's most heavily bombed area. During the 10-year military campaign, the U.S. flew 580,000 bombing missions over Laos, dropping 2 million tons of explosives. More bombs were dropped in Laos during this period then in the entirety of WWII. Perhaps most frightening, of all the bombs that were dropped, 30% or 80 million bomb clusters, remain unexploded and embedded in the Lao countryside.

Although I'm a fiercely patriotic American, during my visit to the *UXO Laos Visitor Center* in Luang Prabang, I was ashamed of my country for the first time. Not only because we dropped the bombs in the first place, but also because we have failed to sign the *International Convention on Cluster Munitions*. This convention bans the use, production, stockpiling, and transfer of cluster munitions and places obligations on countries to clear affected areas, assist victims, and destroy stockpiles. Russia and China have also refused to sign.

In addition to the senseless deaths caused by UXOs, the sheer number of unexploded devices is fueling a rabid industry in scrap metal. Little children, who generally know not to touch the bombs that look like shiny silver baseballs, are now foraging for them anyway. To the kids, who see their parents suffering crushing poverty, these heavy metal objects are a way to earn quick cash, despite the chances of losing a limb or their young life.

To me, this is the quintessential picture of extreme poverty—when a child or a farmer will risk their life to gather unexploded bombs to sell as scrap metal and therefore feed their family.

I was confronted with this terrible dilemma myself in the Laos capital of Vientiane when I bought a bracelet for 10,000 Kip ($1.20). Buying the bracelet was a difficult decision. The woman who sold it to me was sitting on the pavement and handed me a card that read: "Our bracelets are made from aluminum that was part of a plane or bomb dropped on our province during the Secret War. After the war someone taught us what to do with the bombs that destroyed our lives. From bombs we make spoons and bracelets. We make new meaning from the bombs, which help us escape poverty."

I was torn. On one hand, the villagers are doing something productive—creating new industries and sources of income—from the unexploded bombs. On the other hand, this new market for UXOs is encouraging the poor (and many children) to search for the bombs to then sell as scrap metal. While it was a painful decision for me whether or not to buy the bracelet, it pales in comparison with the daily deliberation of the families that are surrounded by these deadly mementos. Do you pick up the UXOs, the explosive dollars, literally lying in your garden?

The poor populations of Cambodia and Laos are still paying a heavy price today for the atrocities committed by governments. It's not only the senseless killing, but the refusal to right a historic wrong, that pains and shames me the most.

Anthony – Livingstone, Zambia

Anthony is someone who has lived through unimaginable pain and has now dedicated his life to helping others. He was introduced to me by my friend Rizwan, whom I met in Cairo. Rizwan had just arrived into town that day and I was leaving the next, so we (Rizwan, his fiancée Angelina, and his couch surfing host Hassan) met for a drink in an English pub in the Egyptian capital.

After a few beers, we moved on to an Arabic café, so we could smoke apricot sheesha and swap stories. Rizwan was just ending his own two-year jaunt around the world and was one of the few people I knew who was traveling and volunteering as I was. He was an invaluable source of advice and introductions as I headed deeper into Africa and he gave me a warm introduction to Anthony.

Originally from Sri Lanka, Anthony has been living in Zambia for more than twenty years. He is super human: running his accounting firm, participating in the local Rotary Club, dedicated to his family, and active in his church.

Anthony also serves as a Director on the board of five nonprofits based in Livingstone. Of these organizations, he founded two: *Lubashi Home*, a residential care facility for Zambian orphans and vulnerable children, and *Lushomo Home*, a home for young girls who have been sexually abused.

My first meeting with Anthony was over breakfast at my campground overlooking the Zambezi River. During our hour-long chat, Anthony was slightly rushed since he had an appointment with the President of Zambia later that morning. Nevertheless, he took great care to describe to me his involvement with each of his charities and their various needs. He also revealed that it was the death of his infant son that impelled him to do his charitable work, particularly his efforts to protect defenseless children.

Anthony's desire to help his organizations was genuine and his enthusiasm contagious. His skills at persuasion were also finely tuned. We decided that I would give a half-day fundraising workshop and visit all five organizations to provide one-on-one consulting. Here's a glimpse of what I got up to.

At the **Youth Community Training Center**, I observed tailoring classes, admired the furniture-making operations, was treated to a lunch prepared by the culinary students, and served by the hospitality class. Most of our business development conversations centered on securing local contracts and quality control issues.

That afternoon I also visited **Mosi-oa-Tunya**, a community radio station run by the Catholic Church. Mosi-oa-Tunya (meaning the "Smoke that Thunders" in reference to the area's mighty Victoria Falls), serves as an outlet for political and cultural discourse throughout much of western Zambia. The station has a huge listenership and we talked about ways to tap this influence by selling on-air advertising.

Anthony was also on the board of **St. Joseph's Hospice**. In Zambia, the average life expectancy is only thirty-eight years, so hospice care is becoming increasingly necessary. St. Joseph's was established as a home for men and women, whom were dying of AIDS and other illnesses. Hospice is where patients, most of whom are poor and have been abandoned by their families, could live in companionship while receiving medical attention and emotional support.

It was at St. Joseph's that I had the pleasure of meeting Sister Amirtha. Of undecipherable age, Sister Amirtha had been sent from her Catholic order of nuns in India to help manage St. Joseph's. I don't believe she had any medical knowledge or management experience, but she was helpful and hopeful and full of faith.

During our conversation she revealed to me that the hospice had only a few weeks of operating funds. I asked her what she was doing about this lack of funding and she answered that she was praying. I asked her again, "What are you *doing* about it?" Sister Amirtha just giggled.

Exploring several options for an immediate cash influx, I suggested she approach the local Catholic Diocese for emergency funding. She told me the church had no money. I whispered to her I had just been to the museums at Vatican City and the church did indeed have money. Again, she giggled.

We sat brainstorming ideas on how to use current assets to raise cash. I suggested that she lease some of the expensive medical equipment, which had been donated and wasn't in use, to local hospitals. Another idea was to have the nursing staff provide healthcare clinics in the community or provide in-home services for a small fee. Sister Amirtha said she thought she would start a mushroom farm. This time, I giggled.

In all my years of consulting I had never heard such a preposterous idea. I asked Sister Amirtha if she had any experience farming? No.

Knowledge of mushrooms? No. Was the soil, from the proposed farmland surrounding the hospice buildings, fertile? No idea.

I was baffled that she wanted to pursue this bizarre business venture. She told me she had read an article online and thought she could tap into the growing demand for mushrooms in Africa. This was my third trip to Africa and I had not noticed such a pent-up appetite for fungi.

I always smile when I think about our exchange that afternoon. I'm still in contact with Sister Amirtha and I know she didn't implement any of my ideas, nor did she go into the mushroom-growing business. And yet the hospice is still in operation. So I guess her strategy of praying worked after all.

Of all of Anthony's organizations doing good work, it was Lushomo Home, the home for sexually abused girls, which struck a chord with me. I was introduced to the Executive Director Christina and the staff, given a tour of their dormitories, and shown the new security gate that was necessary to keep out angry family members. I also got to meet some of the girls, some as young as age seven. It nearly broke my heart to see their shy, smiling faces.

The girls come to Lushomo Home after being removed from their abusive families. It's in this protected haven that they wait for their court cases to come to trial. Usually they never return to their families, but continue to live at Lushomo Home, attending school, and receiving medical care and counseling.

As I continued my travels around the world, the children I met during my time in Livingstone were often in my mind. On a professional level, I find Anthony's dedication and tenacity inspiring. On a personal level,

I share his desire to help and provide for these children, especially the little girls who have suffered horrible pain at the hands of adults.

This commitment to help those who are vulnerable is a reoccurring theme in my own giving. In particular, I like to support organizations that help protect and promote women's and girls' rights. My giving philosophy has evolved over the years and reflects my own history and hopes.

Here's the rationale that shapes my philanthropy:

Philosophical: I believe in inalienable social and civil rights like equality and justice. Feelings of fairness and equal access to opportunity are core to how I see the world and the beliefs that I hold.

Social: There are numerous examples of how gains in women's equality can move whole communities forward. For instance, ending female genital mutilation or "cutting" in some African countries has resulted in an increase in economic activity and prosperity. As women gain greater autonomy and health, they are able to participate more fully in their local economies.

Economic: I prefer to donate to areas that don't receive a large percentage of funding. On average, organizations serving women and girls only receive 7% of all charitable funding in the United States. This relatively low number motivates me to give more to these causes because there is a greater need and I can make a larger impact with a modest donation.

Emotional: Like most women, I have experienced disempowerment first hand, from sexual harassment in the workplace to being a survivor of violence. My personal experiences propel me to fight the discrimination, disenfranchisement, and debasement that many women are subject to on a daily basis.

I try and take this perspective and put it into action. I think it's always better to take risks and participate, then to sit on the sidelines. It's this same philosophy which impels me to travel, to be a woman of motion. To be an Adventure Philanthropist.

My goal is to share what I've learned. That's why I host workshops on international fundraising and organizational growth and provide pro bono consulting when I travel. *I try to* pass along these myriad lessons to other leaders of nonprofit organizations so they can learn from me, from my mistakes, and be better. I look at it as extracting the seeds of hard-won wisdom and replanting them. To see my failures bloom in another, more productive, form.

As he presides over his life changing programs in Livingstone, I think Anthony and I share this same sense of duty: to work on behalf of those who have experienced raw and unrelenting pain. Even if that bounty is only the knowledge that one can survive painful experiences and turn personal hardship into healing.

Mawara & Mafara – Game Reserve, Africa

It was a predictably hot and lazy afternoon at our delta camp, when a group of us visited a local swimming hole. I'd come to Botswana to see the huge abundance of wildlife that are drawn to the Okavango Delta during the dry season, and understood that the swimming hole was a safe place to frolic. As it turns out, it was just a small section that had been cleared of reeds to better spot inquisitive elephants, angry buffalo, or hungry crocodiles.

I got in with the rest of the crew for a quick dip. But between the swishy mud between my toes and my hyper-vigilant watch for movement in the water, I didn't last long. Everyone else seemed to be having a grand time though, splashing and dunking each other, heartily enjoying the cool water in the lush surroundings.

I felt much safer on land or in the confines of our *mokoros*, a type of dug-out canoe carved from a single tree trunk. During our safari, we spent hours in the mokoros, gliding through the reeds on our waterborne safaris. This was one of my favorite experiences of the trip and such a peaceful way to savor the beauty of the Delta up close, see its colorful and small amphibians, and get to know some of the local villagers who captained the canoes and camped out with us. This serene experience was a sharp contrast to what was to come later.

After spending days floating between Delta islands, a few of us wrapped up our safari with a helicopter ride over the Okavango. I thought it would be a perfect way to appreciate the vastness and diversity of the Delta. I was to gain a truly new perspective.

During the half-hour ride, we flew from a high vantage of 500 feet (150 m) to as low as 50 feet (15 m) above the swampy terrain, where we saw bull elephants grazing and magnificent herds of zebra and giraffe. As we swooped down to get a closer sighting of a particularly amazing bull elephant, displaying massive curved tusks, the pilot noted with pity that the elephant would probably be shot the next week. As it turns out, we were camping on a private game reserve (I didn't realize this, I thought we were in a national park) and while they allow tourists to camp and safari on the Delta, the owners also allow big game hunting. NOOOOO!

Our pilot recited the price list for trophy game: $10,000 for a giraffe, $40,000 for a rhino (aren't they nearly extinction?!) and $50,000 for a large bull elephant like the one we were admiring. This handsome animal might be picked off by a single Texan who came back to the Delta to shoot year after year, supposedly using the tusks to build a banister for his staircase.

While the importing of ivory into the U.S. is illegal, there are two improbable loopholes: one for ivory antiques and one for ivory tusk trophies from Africa. When the hunters kill for a souvenir, the local villagers receive the game meat (an elephant can feed the entire village for a number of days) and the reserve owners get a hefty fee. Everyone wins—except the elephant.

It confounds me that in this modern day we continue to wantonly destroy our planet's flora and fauna—even slaughtering endangered animals as a prize. From the plunder of rhino horn for farcical Chinese medicine, to the capture of gorillas and primates for zoos, Africa's precious wildlife is being looted at an alarming rate.

Lion Encounter, a for-profit company that aims to rehabilitate lions back into the wild, reckons that since 1975, Africa has lost between 80-90% of its wild lion population. When I visited their sanctuary in Livingstone, Zambia, I was lucky enough to spend a day with the organization learning more about lions and their dwindling habitat.

The morning started with a rare introduction. I met two eight-month old lion cubs: Mawara and Mafara. Out for an early morning stroll, the twin sisters couldn't have been more different. Mawara (or was it Mafara?) was the gentle one, letting us stroke her as she walked and kneel down to pet her behind her ears. Mafara (or was it Mawara?) was the feisty one. She wouldn't let anyone near her, letting out a little snarl each time one of us got too close.

During our ramble, we got to watch Mafara saunter up to a lake and growl at her reflection at the water's edge. Apparently, by instinct, lions are cautious of the water (think crocodiles), so they usually keep a wide berth from an early age. While Mafara might have been in slight danger from a toothy croc, we tourists never were. Accompanied at all times by a guide, park wardens (with guns), and lion handlers, we also were each given a long stick to distract the lions if necessary.

After the morning walk, I joined a group of volunteers in Mosi-oa-Tunya National Park. All of the volunteers were in residence with Lion Encounter and their sister nonprofit the **African Lion & Environmental Research Trust (ALERT),** were volunteering between a week and two months. I was the only day volunteer and they heartily welcomed me on an anti-poaching snare sweep.

This involved walking in the hot park for several hours, with ten of us spread out at ten-foot intervals searching for wire snares. The wire snares were nearly impossible to see! Most were tied low on spindly tree trunks. The poachers, locals living on the edge of the national park, were hoping to snag an animal's leg or neck in the noose. They would then either eat or sell the wild game. Luckily we didn't find any trapped animals and removed ten empty snares. Ten animals saved!

The final part of my volunteer gig was to help conduct field research, which gave me a chance to learn more about lion behavior firsthand.

A small group of us were loaded into a jeep and driven into the adjacent ALERT reserve, where a pride of six lions had just been released.

Our job as researchers was to watch the lions' every movement. My specific job was to compile an activity report by watching a single lion and note her activity every two minutes. I had a stop watch and a note book and I sat watching attentively...for the first ten minutes.

My lion wasn't actually doing anything. In fact none of the lions were because they had just made a kill the night before and they were still digesting their meal. So our jeep full of research wannabes just watched as the lions lay under the shade of the trees, snoozing the afternoon away. During my one-hour activity report, my lion yawned once, and lifted up her head to look in our direction twice. That was it: three marks in the "activity" notebook.

I actually didn't mind the reprieve, it was a great opportunity to pepper the head researcher with loads of questions about lion behavior. Besides, I got off lucky, especially when you consider some of the other volunteer duties that could have come my way, including meat preparation (chopping up mules with a machete) and enclosure maintenance (picking up poop and gnawed bones).

All in all, it was a really great way to round out my African safari experience, with my volunteer stint allowing me to get close to the animals I had been admiring from afar for weeks. I was also pleased that I got to learn more about the work being done to stop the painful poaching and to meet those working to preserve Africa's incredible natural heritage.

Man of the Forest – Borneo, Malaysia

Another wildlife volunteer experience took me deep into the jungles of Borneo—a magical spot full of indigenous animals, sparkling natural beauty, and constant discovery.

The island of Borneo is home to sixteen million people and comprises three countries: portions of Malaysia, the entire country of Brunei, and portions of Indonesia. While it offers seven distinct eco-systems, including alpine shrubland, peat swamp forests, and mangroves, most of the land is covered by lowland rainforest. This rainforest is the oldest in the world.

I had come to Borneo to specifically see the primates and to dive Sipadan, one of the most venerated dive spots in the world. This exotic island was the place to get my fill of fascinating flora and fauna. I was hoping to see the most famous rainforest resident: the orangutan, translated as "Man of the Forest."

Along with gorillas and chimpanzees, orangutans are a type of great ape that are only found in the rainforests of Sumatra and Borneo. Known for their reddish-brown hair, orangutans live mainly in trees, probably to avoid their biggest predators: tigers and crocodiles. Although at the jungle camp, my guide said that a full-grown python could also take down an orangutan.

Usually solitary, orangutans live to be about thirty years old, and eat a mainly vegetarian diet of fruit, bark, and honey, occasionally supplemented by insects and birds' eggs. One of the most intelligent primates, orangutans use twigs and branches as sophisticated tools to construct intricate nests each day. The nests contain not just a mattress, made by braiding leaves, but pillows and blankets and even bunk beds, all topped with a leafy roof.

My first stop in Borneo was *Sepilok Orang Utan Rehabilitation Centre*. The sanctuary has a small museum, where you can watch an informative video, but the highlight is feeding time, which occurs twice a day. I saw several orangutans visit the feeding platform, both mothers who wanted food for their offspring. I also spotted a couple of orangutans that were transitioning back into the wild, swinging high above in the surrounding trees.

But this wasn't enough for me. I wanted a more authentic Borneo experience, so I booked myself into a jungle camp called Uncle Tan's on the Kinabatangan River. The Kinabatangan is one of only two places on earth where ten primate species can be found together, including orangutan, proboscis monkey, macaques, maroon langur, and Bornean gibbon, all of which are endemic to Borneo.

One of the reasons I chose Uncle Tan's was because of the camp's commitment to protecting the environment. The lodge had a small reforestation project which employs local village youth to help replant trees along a stretch of riverbank bordering the camp. I wandered over one afternoon to help plant the tender tree shoots.

While at the camp, I stayed in one of the open huts (thatched roof, wood walls, no doors) with Teruko, another solo female traveler from Japan. We both had our own flea and bed bug-infested mattress (Oh no, not again!), placed on a raised wooden floor, and covered with a filthy mosquito net. Ahhhh...Here was my "authentic" experience.

The entire camp was built on stilts as the river frequently floods the banks. In fact, the day before we arrived, the wooden walkways were all under water. There were long-drop toilets a short walk away and a chance to take river-water bucket showers so you could wash away your sweat with brown river water. I was not tempted.

Honestly, the camp was a bit wild. A couple from the Netherlands couldn't hack it and left immediately, but Teruko and I toughed it out. It didn't even bother us that rats had chewed a hole in Teruko's backpack one the night. Although there was no food in the backpack (we placed all edible items in a sealed plastic bucket), the rats were attracted to the smell of sweat from Teruko's dirty clothes. Supremely disgusting.

A brood of young guys ran the camp and were good fun. They sang and played the guitar at night, gave us cooking lessons, and every day, in the late morning, they hosted a soccer game against the local fishermen, who called themselves *Orang Sungei* or "River People." This friendly game of camp staff and tourists versus locals was intense. Running around in real football uniforms and plastic cleats, it was obviously the highlight of everyone's day.

We packed a lot in during our time at the camp, with sunrise and sunset boat safaris on the river, jungle walks during the day, and swamp walks at night. We saw monkeys, bats, and many of Borneo's gorgeous birds. My favorite was the bizarre proboscis monkeys, which have an enormous schnoz. It's literally as big as a grown man's hand and protrudes from the center of their face, hanging down like a limp sack over their upper lip. They're actually quite cute, in an ugly-sort-of-way.

On our nightly swamp walks, we waded through knee-high waters searching for pythons in the dark trees or swimming through the murky black water. Did I mention that pythons have been known to reach 19 feet (nearly 6 m) in length? Let's be frank, I was relieved that we didn't see any and during the night I remained on high alert in our open-air huts for any slithering sounds. I'm not much bigger than an orangutan, you know.

On one of our sunset safaris we were lucky enough to see three Men of the Forest industriously building their nests in the shoreline trees. While the orangutans were in the distance, my powerful camera lens provided a good sighting. We also spied their silhouettes between the tree limbs as they climbed about, their distinctive red hair glowing in the setting sun.

Sadly, the Borneo population has decreased by more than 50% and the Sumatran orangutan is critically endangered. This road to extinction is paved by the palm oil industry which is destroying the orangutan's habitat through deforestation. Malaysia dominates the palm oil market with a 45% share of worldwide production.

Palm oil accounts for 30% of all edible plant oil used in cooking and foodstuffs, including most cookies, crackers, popcorn, frozen dinners, candy, ice cream, and, of course, fast food. Somewhat surprisingly, palm oil is also an ingredient found in most beauty products, including soap, shampoo, and cosmetics.

One way you can make a difference without even leaving town is to ask manufacturers of your favorite brands to make corporate donations to help preserve the remaining rainforests in Borneo. There's also civic action. The Girl Scouts just discontinued the use of palm oil in their cookies after one of its young scouts started a petition. Go Girl Scouts!

The World Wildlife Fund's *Heart of Borneo* campaign is working along the same lines, asking companies that purchase timber and palm oil from Borneo to only buy goods from sustainable sources. Other initiatives have started working with local communities to help develop alternative sources of income, to reduce the economic pressure on Borneo's remarkable habitat and to provide a reprieve to the primary victims: the gentle men of the forest.

From the treetops to the ocean floor, Borneo is suffering unparalleled environmental degradation. I witnessed the full spectrum of abasement as I journeyed from my jungle camp to the island of Mabul, about an hour boat ride from the eastern Malaysian coastline.

Mabul is the closest island to the world renowned dive spot, Sipadan, and the only place for divers to stay. My budget didn't allow me to stay at the resorts, so I opted for a local version: a traditional Malaysian long house. This turned out to be a great decision.

I stayed at a family-owned long house called Arung Hayat. "Arung" means sea nymph and "Hayat" is the name of the family's beloved aunt. I paid just $30 a night for a single room with my own bath and full board. It was pretty basic, but clean, and there was plenty of good food, eaten family style.

Most importantly, Hanif and Dandy and all the guys at Arung Hayat made me feel right at home, sharing their rum and songs every night. Dandy also took me around to see bits of the island, like a band playing at another dive resort. We even attended a local island wedding. With no internet access nor electricity after 6:00 pm, you're pretty cut off. I did a couple of dives each day, hung out on the beach, and read. Bliss!

I also explored the island proper, visiting local schools and checking out the sea gypsy villages. Sea gypsies are boat people who migrate between islands. They're illegal immigrants and usually live an "outsider" type of life, meaning their kids don't attend school, they trade for what they need, and sell fish to passing boats to survive. They're not quite pirates, but they're renegades and have a rogue reputation.

Some sea gypsies never set foot on land but live with their family on a small wooden boat, washing in the ocean, and going to the bathroom hanging over the side of the boat. But on Mabul, the sea gypsies have also come ashore and live in ramshackle shacks, either precariously perched above the seawater on stilts or situated right on the shoreline.

The gypsy villages, with their lack of plumbing and electricity, stood in stark contrast to the five-star resorts only a few steps away. The unkempt island kids play in the sand underneath the huts, tossing about rotten fruit and drawing pictures in the dirt. As I wandered about, I was far more intrigued by the gypsy flotsam, rather than the sanitized purity of the luxury hotels.

Unfortunately, there was much to hold my attention. While the island is beautiful, trash is starting to choke the beaches and corrupt the ocean floor. In fact, the waters right under our long house were filled with debris and "cigar fish," since without indoor plumbing, most locals simply use long-drop toilets that empty directly into the ocean.

One outfit that regularly performs beach clean ups is *Scuba Junkie*. Situated on the fancy end of Mabul, the proprietors regularly enlist the help of divers and school kids to pick up trash. The day I participated, there were ten of us divers and about twenty local kids. Our beach clean-up didn't really make a dent in all the trash, but their participation is beginning to build awareness with the next generation of island dwellers.

Another trend that is harming the marine life of the island is blast fishing, a practice that uses explosives to stun or kill whole schools of fish. While it's illegal in many countries, its use is sadly widespread off the coasts of Africa and the oceans surrounding Southeast Asia, particularly the Philippines and Indonesia.

The blasts indiscriminately kill all marine life, even destroying the delicate ecosystem that supports the marine habitat, such as coral reefs. This short-sighted practice is killing the rival economy of the island: dive tourism. With coral reefs taking at least ten years to re-establish themselves, this is a trend that will have long-term repercussions for these fishing villages.

I found this type of careless destruction painful to witness, how mercenaries are decimating our rainforests, marine ecosystems, and endangered species. This environmental destruction, coupled with the thoughtless disregard for human life, especially children, pains me.

In the end, it is the innocent and pure—children, animals, our environment—that are sacrificed to the gluttony of others. Greedy businesses are killing the lush flora and fauna of Southeast Asia. Greedy hunters are killing off the precious wildlife in Africa. And greedy consumers are inadvertently helping to destroy entire habitats by creating a market for damaging industries. Greed and destruction are two sides of the same corrupt coin and the cause of most of my pain and anguish. It's unbearable to watch purity destroyed for the profit of others.

Chapter 9: **LOVE**

Love is hard to define. More complicated than simply sexual desire or passion, love may be more akin to a deep affection that one person feels toward another—family members, a child, a friend, or a pet. It's a potent tonic, blending devotion and sacrifice and respect.

I believe my travels brought me closer to the many different forms that love can take. That said, no one's more surprised than me that this chapter on "Love" starts with a discussion of rodents and ends with a story about reptiles, but there you are.

Ziko the Rat – Mozambique

I love my rat Ziko. Ziko is a Giant African Pouched Rat who lives and works in Mozambique. Known as a "HEROrat," he has been trained to detect land mines left behind in war-torn countries. I've sponsored Ziko for a number of years, paying $7 a month to help pay for his welfare and training.

I receive quarterly updates with pictures and information about Ziko, so I kinda feel like I know the dude. For instance, Ziko was born on March 30, 2008 and he comes from a family of five, very large by rat standards. His father Thomas is a demining rat and his mother is from the wild. In turn, Ziko and his wife Zuma have three children: Savanna, Muchanna, and Jobbary. They are all in the demining training program. I hear Ziko's personality is calm and focused and he's eager to do his job well. That's the kind of rat I like.

I was on my way to meet Ziko in person, traveling overland from Zambia to Mozambique when I opted to evacuate in Malawi. When political turmoil forced me to cut my Malawi adventure short, I missed my chance to meet Ziko. This was one of the greatest disappointments I had during my trip. I was so looking forward to seeing the demining operations and holding my rat friend.

HEROrats *is* one of my favorite programs and is run by a Belgian nonprofit called **APOPO**, which researches, develops, and implements detection-rat technology for humanitarian purposes, such as mine action and tuberculosis detection. APOPO has several hundred rats in various stages of breeding, training, research, and operations.

Unfortunately Ziko and his co-workers are busy. At present, more than 100 million landmines are deployed in more than 90 countries around the world. Landmines kill or maim between 40-55 people per day, which means every 20 minutes, someone is hurt or killed by a landmine.

The Mozambique civil war alone left an estimated 500,000 landmines planted throughout the country. APOPO is working as part of the National Demining Program of Mozambique, which is committed to ridding the country of its landmine legacy by 2014. As part of this project, APOPO cleared nearly 26 million square feet (8 million sq m) of land in 1 province alone, finishing a year ahead of schedule. The organization has now been given 3 additional provinces to clear.

What I like about the APOPO's program is that when they remove the physical danger of landmines, they are subsequently releasing the land for productive use. So de-mining makes communities safer, while improving economic prospects and environmental conditions. Now can you see why I love this rat?

There are many advantages to using rats to detect mines. One is speed. A HEROrat can clear a landmine field in thirty minutes, which is the equivalent of two days' work for a human de-miner. In addition, rats are too lightweight to trip the mines, so they stay alive even after detection. The rats are trained to pause or scratch on the surface when they have found an active mine.

Other benefits of rodent-dom include rats' terrific sense of smell, which helps them to detect both metal and plastic-cased explosives. Rats are also highly intelligent and easy to train. Lastly, rats are abundant, small (easy to transport), and live a long time, so the organization can count on many years of productivity.

Based on the tremendous success of its demining programs, APOPO is now using rats to detect Tuberculosis (TB). An untreated TB patient can infect a further dozen people per year, so there's a crucial need for faster TB detection, especially in crowded cities.

Working in labs, HEROrats smell sputum samples and screen them for TB. One rat can evaluate more samples in ten minutes, than a lab technician can do in a day. Using rats also helps reduce the lab technicians' exposure to the disease. In this way, rats are instrumental to helping eradicate TB in Sub-Saharan Africa. Love it!

Another of my favorite rodents is **Big Brother Mouse**, the face and name of a nonprofit organization based in Luang Prabang, Laos. Since 2006, Big Brother Mouse has been publishing books in the Lao language and distributing books to communities. Their goal is to show children that reading can be fun.

With an average annual income in Laos of about $500, a book is considered a luxury. In addition, books published in the Lao language are rare. As a result, many children have never read a book outside of school textbooks.

While visiting the Big Brother Mouse bookstore, I was curious to see some of the titles that have been translated into Lao and what Lao children are reading. Universal children's stories reign, including *Dr. Doolittle, The Tale of Peter Rabbit, Pinocchio, The Monkey King,* and my favorite *The Diary of Anne Frank.* The bookstore also stocks plenty of local Lao folklore, Lao-language coloring books, and books about community health.

One way Big Brother Mouse helps to spread the joy of reading is by hosting book parties, where children receive the gift of a book—usually the first book they've ever owned—and by starting mini-libraries, where children can swap their book for a new one. In 2012, more than 125,000 rural Lao children received a book through a Big Brother Mouse book party.

I tried to volunteer at the Big Brother Mouse reading center several times. But each time I went, there were more of us language exchange teachers than there were students, so I decided to support the organization by promoting it through my monthly Donate My Dollars poll. That month, I gave a $350 donation to host a book party and challenged the GoErinGo.com readers to vote "yes" for more books. We received the necessary 150 votes, triggering an additional $150 donation from my fund—enough to provide a new mini-library too!

On October 4, 2011, Big Brother Mouse hosted the GoErinGo-sponsored book party in the village of Ban Pakseuang. During the 3-hour party, the children celebrated all-things book, participating in readings, songs, art lessons, and games. At the end, each child got to choose his / her first book to take home with them! In addition, the grant paid for a part-time librarian to run the new lending library, which houses 250 books for the children of Ban Pakseuang to enjoy.

If you'd like to encourage reading in Laos, you can sponsor your own book party and lending library, pay for a book translation, donate surplus books, or grant Big Brother Mouse the Lao-language publishing rights to your own book.

On my end, I'll be granting the rights of this book to Big Brother Mouse in case they want to make it available for young adult readers in rural villages. The granting of publishing rights seems like a fitting way to share my love of reading with a new generation ready to explore the places that stories can take you.

Mummy Bev – Kathmandu, Nepal

Perhaps the strongest love is a mother's unconditional affection for her child. Although I'm not a mother, I can recognize this intensity in the parents I know and I feel it emanating from my own mother. On my journey I met many mothers who were striving to provide loving homes for their children, biological or not. One of these women of deep affection is my friend Beverly.

I originally met Beverly when we were both living in New York City. I was thinking about volunteering with her, and although we didn't work together at the time, I remembered her work with children in Nepal. I contacted her as soon as I knew my travels would take me in her direction.

"Mummy Bev," as she's known by the children she cares for, is the founder of a children's home called *Ghar Sita Mutu*, Nepali for "House with Heart," based in the capital Kathmandu. What I love so much about her story is that she's proof that a regular, everyday person with an open heart can choose to make a world of difference in the lives of those who are most vulnerable, like destitute women and abandoned children.

Beverly is a mother of two and a trained social worker. She originally traveled to Nepal from the U.S. to attend a meditation and yoga retreat. Each day on her way to her practice, she passed by a mother and two little boys sitting on the side of the street. One afternoon, as she passed by she noticed the mother was gone. She had abandoned her two little boys, Krishna and Babu, ages five and two, and left them huddled together outside a tin hut.

Unable to find anyone to care for the children, Beverly became their guardian and enrolled the children in a boarding school when it was time for her to return home. Unfortunately, the boys didn't thrive in the bleak school and Beverly began dreaming of a way she could provide a permanent home for them and for other abandoned children in the city.

After some initial fundraising and a financial commitment from friends, Beverly returned to Nepal and rented a twelve-room house. Ghar Sita Mutu had officially opened its doors. Several years later, Beverly raised enough money to purchase land and convert a derelict carpet factory into a new home. This permanent space provided housing for twenty children and local staff.

Unfortunately the abandonment of children like Krishna and Babu is not uncommon in Nepal, nor in other poverty-stricken areas of the world. Some estimate that there are more than 60 million abandoned children and infants globally. In Nepal, children are often forced into bonded labor or are found fending for themselves, living on the streets. A minimum of 12,000 women and children are trafficked from Nepal to India each year.

The problem of child abandonment is a social one in Nepal. Nepali men often have multiple families and refuse to marry women with children from another man. As we mentioned, illiteracy is high, especially for women. So if a husband leaves his wife, the woman has no way to support herself and her children. One of the few ways out of her predicament is to abandon her children, freeing herself to remarry.

Understanding the plight of Nepal's uneducated and unskilled women, Beverly soon expanded Ghar Sita Mutu's services to help provide destitute women with job training. Her job training center teaches women sewing, felt-making, and knitting skills to improve their employment prospects and opportunity for independence. In addition, Ghar Sita Mutu helps neighborhood families by paying for school tuition and books, providing mother-child wellness care, and offering free childcare for working mothers.

When I arrived in Nepal, I met up with Beverly in Thamel, Kathmandu's famed backpacker grotto. As we ate lunch, we decided that I would volunteer with Beverly when I returned to Kathmandu after my Annapurna trek.

When I returned several weeks later, Beverly and I rolled up our sleeves and worked together to create a fundraising development plan for the organization. We brainstormed ways to leverage Ghar Sita Mutu's global support bases in Hong Kong, London, and the U.S. Our objective was to create specific strategies that could bring in more funding to solidify, diversify, and expand the organization's programs. In short, I had my consulting hat on.

I produced an abbreviated plan highlighting numerous ways the organization could tap both individual and institutional donors, then wrote a number of fundraising vehicles for Ghar Sita Mutu to use. These included a letter of inquiry, a two-page organizational overview, and recruitment communications to help formalize a network of global advisors. This is typical of the way I often volunteer with organizations around the world.

Also typical is the real insight I gained from working closely with Beverly, meeting the women and seeing the job training classes up-close, and being surrounded by formerly disadvantaged children who are now flourishing.

This is the real reward of volunteering—to be able to donate my time and skills as a professional fundraiser to help increase resources so that Beverly and others can continue to do their good work. For me, this is not only about understanding complex social issues, but also about contributing to their solutions.

Another benefit of volunteering is getting the inside track to places I might not normally see. For instance, Beverly arranged for me to stay at a monastery on the outskirts of the city, in Boudha, home to the famed Boudhanath, the largest *stupa* in Nepal and the holiest Tibetan Buddhist temple outside Tibet.

With Tibet almost inaccessible, Boudhanath is one of the few places in the world where you can see a thriving Tibetan culture. Daily prayer services are held in more than fifty surrounding *gompas* (monasteries), and at sun set, the local community, including many maroon-robed monks, turn out to circumambulate the shine, an ancient ritual that is equal parts religious observance and social interaction.

Many of Nepal's population of 20,000 Tibetan are exiles that left the country during China's illegal annexation of this sovereign nation in 1950. In the last five years, a further 2,500-3,500 Tibetans have fled their country, crossing the mountainous border from Tibet into Nepal on foot. The United Nations High Commissioner for Refugees is tasked with monitoring, collecting data, and educating border security personnel on the safe passage afforded to Tibetans as they move through Nepal en route to India. Yet despite these safeguards,

Nepali border patrols routinely deport Tibetan refugees back to the area controlled by China.

I observed the lives of exiled Tibetans while visiting one of three refugee camps in the city of Pokhara. My friends and I went to support these displaced people, who earn a living by selling traditional Tibetan crafts, particularly beautifully hand-woven carpets, as well as jewelry. I did my bit by buying a much loved hand-beaded Tibetan necklace. While my friends were perusing the carpets on offer, I struck up a conversation with a man who was born in the camp and has lived there all his life.

He belongs to a generation of Tibetans in exile who face a crisis of identity. If he leaves the camp and obtains full Nepali citizenship, he feels he will have abandoned his Tibetan heritage. If he remains as a refugee, he is only tangentially recognized by the Nepali government, which restricts his ability to travel, limits his access to healthcare, and curtails his civil rights. So while he remains in the camp, he is, in essence, state-less. There are tens of thousands of Tibetans living in this same political and social limbo. People without a home.

The *International Campaign for Tibet* is a nonprofit that is monitoring the situation of Tibetan refugees, gathering and disseminating first-hand information. They help to ensure safe passage and humanitarian assistance for Tibetans, advocate for Tibetan rights, and try to secure the release and humane treatment of all monks, nuns, and laypeople who have been detained.

Spending a full month in Nepal and volunteering with Beverly helped me learn about the people that live there, both local Nepali and Tibetan refugees, and the poverty and indignities they suffer.

The more I saw, the more I understood one of the main tenets of Buddhism: Everything in this world is interconnected.

The Buddhist symbol for interconnected is the infinity knot, a line without a beginning or an end. The infinity knot is a symbol of the god Vishnu's unending love for his consort Lakshmi, and is also symbolic of the Buddha's infinite compassion.

Perhaps it's fitting then, that on the morning of my departure, Beverly presented me with a thank you gift: a beautiful inlaid silver pendant in the form of the endless knot that ties us all together. The gift was certainly a symbol—of both the intertwining of wisdom and compassion on the cosmic level, and a symbol of our friendship and mutual respect here in the terrestrial world. I love the gift and everything that it represents of my time in Nepal.

This idea of interconnectedness is core to us Adventure Philanthropists. It's why we voluntarily share what we have—time, energy, money or knowledge—with those who may benefit. It's at the heart of the way we choose to inhabit, to discover, our world. This connection that strengthens us all, and that we seek to share, just might be called love.

Uncle Anura – Kandy, Sri Lanka

My personal friendships open the door to many of my volunteering opportunities while on the road. For instance, introductions through my friend Utthama, an American of Sri-Lankan descent now living in Colombo, paved the way for me to visit two children's homes in Sri Lanka; one in the capital, and another in the lake-side town of Kandy.

The children in these homes received very different levels of care and presented me with a complex giving decision.

The orphanage in Colombo, located on the outskirts of the city, provides a home for twenty-five young girls. It was originally founded by a prosperous local family and now was being run by the older generation of aunts and uncles. I was invited by one of the cousins to see if I could help breathe new life into the organization.

I began my visit by touring the girls' home. When I arrived, the girls were playing cricket with rough sticks in the dusty courtyard, yelling enthusiastically as some of the stronger girls sent the ball searing toward the back wall. The best batter was a girl in her early teens, who'd been found homeless, wandering the streets of Colombo. At first, she had trouble adapting to life at the orphanage, frequently acting out against the house mothers and other girls. Slowly, with a chance to put down some roots, she was starting to adapt to her new surroundings.

Her life in the home, and the lives of her new sisters, is certainly better than a precarious life on the streets. The girls have the basic necessities. They sleep in their own beds, eat regularly, go to school. A local dance teacher comes in several times a week to volunteer and teach the girls traditional Sri Lankan songs and dance. I got to peek in at the girls learning to be graceful with their lean bodies. And saw their colorful collages, remnants from a recent art show, adorning the halls of the home. I bought several of the paintings, asking each girl to autograph her artwork.

After meeting these lovely young ladies, I was sadden to see the desperate state of their living conditions. The indoor plumbing was in a chronic state and the outside showers were nothing more than a faucet with a sheet of plastic to give the girls privacy from the prying eyes of neighbors. The girls' rooms were sweltering in the tropical heat, but the fans weren't working, despite Utthama and her families' donation of new ones only months before. Either they weren't installed properly or the electricity had been shut off.

It was readily apparent that the place had fallen into disrepair and urgently needed an infusion of funds. I offered to give a workshop and to work one-on-one with several Board of Directors. While the younger cousins were more open to the idea, the older generation, who still retains control over the home, didn't agree to meet. This was a huge disappointment to me.

Their decision, and the fact that the home is run by a family trust of a wealthy merchant, made it hard for me to give more than I did. I feel it's the trust's fiduciary responsibility to provide a rich and nourishing environment for the children under their care. Most frustrating is that the members of the Board have the financial resources, but were denying the girls under their care the same amenities that they lavish on their own children. This was hard for me to accept.

This grim scenario stood in stark contrast to the children's home that I visited later that month in the hill country town of Kandy. I was introduced to **Singithi Sevana**, which means "Children's Rest," by Utthama's uncle Anura, who sits on the Board of Directors. The organization was originally founded by a local doctor, Dr. Wejesundera, and is now run by his widow Manel.

I met Manel one night in her home and she told me about her late-husband's generosity. Dr. Wejesundera, working in the local hospital, was distressed to see children being abandoned in the waiting room by their families. He created Singithi Sevana as a safe place where the discarded children could be raised.

The home currently cares for thirty-two orphaned or needy children, between two to twelve years of age. The younger children attend a preschool at the home, conducted by a trained teacher, while the older children attend state-run primary and secondary schools in Kandy. The children are given extra lessons in English, math, and music.

Uncle Anura took me on a tour of the facilities and I appreciated the high standards of maintenance and cleanliness throughout the classrooms and living spaces. I was particularly impressed by the kitchen and washing up areas, which were designed specifically for children, with sinks lowered to accommodate their small statures. The surrounding yard featured a composting project and a two-acre garden. The garden helps provide fresh vegetables for the children, as well as generating additional income for the home.

While talking with Manel, she mentioned that the children's beds needed new mattresses. Remembering that Singithi Sevana actually means "Children's Rest," I thought this was the perfect donation. So the GoEringo! Fund granted $600 to cover the cost of new beds for the children. I loved being able to provide a good night's sleep for all the little ones.

Incidentally, Singithi Sevana also turned down my offer to help them learn how to tap funding in the U.S. But declined help is part of volunteering. Many times, the way we volunteers wish to donate our skills isn't either needed or appreciated. When this happens, I try and offer the support that the organization is seeking. Like the new mattresses.

As my two contrasting experiences in Sri Lanka show, who we chose to help can be an agonizing decision for a donor. Do I help the children who (arguably) need the funding more at the poorly run home? Or do I help the children at the home that is being properly managed? It's not a straightforward choice.

When I have to make tough decision like this, I recall a question my Australian friend Sharon asked me years earlier as we floated down the River Nile in Egypt: "Why do you give money when you can't possibly make a difference?" My answer: "While I can't solve the world's problems, I can alleviate a little bit of suffering. And I'm happy to do so." During my travels in Sri Lanka, I was able to help in a very small way. At least I was able to give some children the sweet dreams they deserve.

As I made my way from Kandy to one of Sri Lanka's most famous spots, the colonial-era town of Nuwara Eliya, I was in search of my own peaceful slumber. Here I stayed at the plush Nuwara Eliya Golf Club, thanks to Uncle Anura, who vouched for me as his guest. By the time I got there, I was certainly in need of a comfortable bed.

As I often do, I decided to travel by public bus. Now, this was one of the most crowded buses I had ever been on (which is saying something) and adding to my distress, I needed to go to the bathroom badly and there was no relief in sight. Furthermore, I was badly harassed at the bus station. While I was trying to transfer buses, several insistent men wanted to take me places I didn't want to go.

I had originally intended to stop in Hatton and take part in the night-time pilgrimage to the base of *Sri Pada*, or "Adam's Peak," the highest mountain in Sri Lanka. This sacred place is revered by Buddhists, Hindus, Muslims, and Christians alike.

Buddhists believe that the rock formation near the Sri Pada summit is Buddha's sacred footprint. Tamil Hindus consider it to be the footprint of Lord Shiva. Muslims and Christians believe it's the footprint of Adam, the first placed he stepped in this world. Still others believe that the summit is the place where butterflies go to die. (I like this last one!)

Unfortunately, I never made it to Sri Pada. Instead, I sat festering in a minivan that had about forty people packed in. I was lucky enough to have a seat with my big backpack in front of me and my small backpack on my lap. I was also by the window which helped keep claustrophobia at bay since I had a small stream of fresh air. So really, I had it pretty good.

Everyone was crammed so tight that several arms were literally covering my eyes and brushing my face as the other standing passengers were leaning forward trying to hold on to the side of the careening van. Did I mention it was nearly 105 °F (40 °C)? An hour into the 3-hour ride, it took all my restraint not to start screaming and biting the fleshy arms in front of me.

I nearly let loose with a Grade A foreigner freak-out. How did I hold it together? I realized that if I had a tantrum I would simply be dumped on the side of the road to wait for another equally crowded minivan to pick me up. By taking a deep breath and regaining my composure, I was able to further restrain myself and my bladder, but just barely.

Even on the verge of my melt down, I still had the wherewithal to feel incredibly ashamed of my intolerance of the situation. The people stuffed with me in the van were all Tamil tea pickers, dressed up for their night on the town after six days of picking tea leaves in the sticky Sri Lankan sun. If anyone deserved a good night's sleep it was this group of manual laborers, helping bring the joys of tea to the world.

Sri Lanka, previously known as Ceylon, is one of the world's largest tea exporters. Tea production accounts for 15% of the country's GDP and employs more than 1 million people. My main purpose of visiting Nuwara Eliya was to check out life on the tea plantations.

The plantation I visited had 1,400 employees, including 800 women pickers. The pickers were paid a straight salary to pick 35 lbs (16 kg) during an 8-hour work day. If they picked more than the required amount, they earned a bonus.

I walked through the tea trails and found women in small groups picking bags of tea. The bags were strapped across their foreheads to help carry the heavy load. For a tip, they let me film their flying fingers and posed for photos. I was happy to give them the extra income.

Sri Lanka's Sinhalese population was reticent about working on the plantations, so Tamils from southern India were brought to the Hill Country to work in the fields. A large proportion of the workers are young women; the minimum age for joining the ranks is twelve. Traditionally, young girls follow their mothers, grandmothers, and older sisters onto the picking trail.

The young women live in housing "lines," attached houses with just one or two rooms. As many as ten laborers live in one room, most without windows. Since the women and girls have no privacy from the male laborers, sexual harassment, discrimination, and victimization are rife. But things are beginning to change. More than eighty-five neighborhood women's groups have been formed across Sri Lanka, helping educate plantation workers about gender equality, leadership, and preventing violence against women.

While the tea pickers endure a daily grind, the whole of Sri Lanka endured tragedy during the 2004 Boxing Day tsunami. The Asian tsunami disaster claimed 35,000 lives and displaced more than 1 million people living on Sri Lanka's coastline. As you drive up the western side of the island, you see the beautiful beaches dotted with grave markers, memorials to those who perished in the waters that day.

Near the town of Peraliya, about 60 miles (95 km) south of Colombo, stands a monument to those who died in the tragedy. A towering white Buddha marks the place where a train, the "Queen of the Sea," was derailed by the giant wave. The crash left almost all 1,200 passengers dead and is considered the worst rail accident in history. More than 8 years after the disaster, Sri Lankans living on the coast are still rebuilding their lives.

I stopped at the memorial to pay my respects before I reached my ultimate destination: Kosgoda, home to a turtle hatchery. **Kosgoda Sea Turtle Conservation Project** is working to reverse the tide that signals the end for marine turtles. After plying the oceans for 190 million years, only eight species of marine reptiles are living today.

The beaches of Sri Lanka are nesting grounds for five of these species: the Green Turtle, Leatherback, Hawksbill, Loggerhead, and the Olive Ridley. While all turtles and their products are protected by international law, the market for turtle meat and shells in Sri Lanka is still lucrative, despite anyone in the possession of turtle products being hit with a jail sentence and fines.

Fighting for the preservation of turtles are 18 hatcheries found along Sri Lanka's western and southern coasts. During just a 3-year period, they hatched nearly 100,000 sea turtles and released them to the sea. A key to the hatcheries' success is a program that pays local fishermen for eggs that they collect at night along the sandy beach. The hatcheries pay fishermen a few cents more than they can get at the local market. The hatcheries then re-bury the eggs in the warm sand and hope that they hatch.

During my visit to the Kosgoda hatchery, I saw huge tanks filled with newborn hatchlings. I also learned all I could about sea turtles, including how they breathe (coming up for air every 30 minutes), reproduce (laying 80-120 eggs on the beach in the same spot they themselves were hatched), and where they go (anywhere they want—a Leatherback turtle tagged in South America was recovered off the coast of West Africa!)

When they hatch, the young turtles make their way straight to sea and swim constantly for up to 2 days. This is known as the "juvenile frenzy" and allows the young turtles to escape the predator-rich inshore waters. Although less than 10% of the baby turtles will survive, it's inspiring to know that hatcheries all over Sri Lanka are helping improve the odds.

At the hatcheries, the turtle hatchlings are kept and fed an average of three days. After this strengthening period, the baby turtles are taken to the sea and released, usually under the cover of darkness. I went to Kosgoda to help release the turtles at dusk.

Me and a handful of other volunteers placed the little guys on the sand facing the waves and cheered them on as they made the perilous journey out to sea. Their first obstacle was a man-made one: a gaggle of drunk guys playing American football with a bottle of rum were blocking their way. I took it upon myself to issue a few tackles of my own. No one's going to block these baby turtles on my watch! See, a mother's love is strong (even if it's only for teeny tiny turtles).

Releasing the turtle hatchlings at sunset on the beach in Sri Lanka is one of the best memories I have from my trip. The renewed chance at life for the hatchlings is uplifting, as is the second chance that the abandoned children in orphanages are receiving. This opportunity to help provide children and communities with a better future is heartening and it's the reason why my definition of love includes mattresses and motherhood, rodents and reptiles.

Chapter 10: **GRATITUDE**

There was so much to be thankful for on my two-year trek. Honestly, it's hard to know where to begin. The people I met and places I discovered, the experiences I shared. Sometimes, I can't believe that I've been so fortunate to have been able to experience the world at such a deep, visceral level. Not just to see what I never could have imagined, but also to *feel* emotions I never thought I would.

If nothing else, my two years of traveling alone around the world gave me the opportunity to experience the raw emotion that many people shy away from. I can honestly say, I never felt more intensely alive.

My map of the world is now different, not just a collection of cities, but a plaid of people's faces, who have touched and changed me forever. I'd like to introduce you to three people on my map who provided me with this heady combination—novel places, unexplored cultures, a chance to learn and to help give back. I am eternally grateful for these friendships.

PT Pirjo – Finnish Lapland

I flew to Helsinki and took an internal flight north to Rovaniemi, and then a 3-hour bus ride way the hell up there. We're talking Lapland.

I went to meet my friend Pirjo, a 50-year old physical therapist who lives in the small town of Sodankylä, 200 miles inside the Arctic Circle. This far north, the temperature can be a pleasant 80° F (26° C) in summer, but in the winter, a not-so-pleasant -80° F (-62° C). That's a minus sign.

Rovaniemi is interesting because it's where Santa Claus lives. If you or your children have ever written a letter to Santa and addressed it to the North Pole, it ends up in the hands of the good people of Rovaniemi, Finland. It's a town that thrives on the Santa-tourism industry.

I originally met Pirjo while hiking in the Himalayas. She was one of the five women on our twelve-day trek to Annapurna Base Camp. As a physical therapist, she was certainly handy to have on the trail. By the end of the trek, I was slipping her Snickers bars in exchange for expert leg wraps every morning to shore up my fragile knees.

Like a lot of Finns, Pirjo was quiet on the trek, but exhibited a sly sense of humor once she warmed up. And she was strong. And she could eat a lot of potatoes. Boy, could she eat potatoes!

Pirjo was in Nepal for the second time, volunteering at a hospital in Kathmandu. She was charged $15 a day to cover her food and accommodation, which was very basic, but right in the vicinity of the hospital so she could walk to work. I remember her telling me stories of how she did all her laundry by hand in the sink and took cold bucket showers for the full 3 months.

As a physical therapist, Pirjo specializes in treating leprosy patients, so she volunteered at a hospital started more than 50 years ago by an organization called *The Leprosy Mission International* (TLMI). Today, the hospital is run by Nepali medical staff, while still receiving some financial support and staff training from TLMI.

TLMI supports a community-based healthcare model focusing on prevention and rehabilitation, as well as education and advocacy. Because leprosy affects people's lives in many different ways, they seek to care for patients' physical, social, spiritual, and psychological needs.

Globally, there are still nearly three million people with leprosy-related disabilities. And while some countries have eradicated leprosy, the disease has become entrenched in India, Indonesia, and Brazil, and is spreading in Bangladesh, Myanmar, Nigeria, and Nepal. In fact, every two minutes a person is diagnosed with Hansen's disease. So unfortunately, Pirjo's skills and experience are much in demand.

Being a taciturn Finn, it took me several weeks to uncover the full extent of Pirjo's volunteering experience. Her first volunteer engagement was a year spent in Bhutan and now, every two years, she arranges to take a six-month sabbatical to volunteer abroad. Pirjo has found a way to incorporate overseas volunteering into her life, leveraging her professional skills to help train fellow health professionals in other countries. A primo Adventure Philanthropist!

Not only was I grateful to climb alongside Pirjo through the Himalayas (spoiled by having a physical therapist by my side), but I so enjoyed extracting her stories of volunteer life in Bhutan and Nepal. And, of course, I was grateful that she asked me to visit her in Finland after our trek.

In my mind, when someone invites you to Finnish Lapland, you go. So before we left our hiking base camp in Pokhara, Nepal, I arranged to meet up with Pirjo later that summer to spend the longest days of the year at her family's cottage deep in the Arctic Circle. Here I would have a true Finnish experience. Hot diggity!

Finding my way to Lapland turned into a small trial and I found myself in an empty parking lot in the town of Inari, a stone's throw from the Russian border. This was not where I was supposed to be. I called Pirjo and she told me to get on another bus and backtrack four hours. Apparently I had blown right by the town of Sodankylä where I was supposed to disembark. I actually noticed that the bus stopped thereabouts, but I thought it was only a rest stop, not the region's second largest town. Oops.

I finally made it back to the pick-up point, where Pirjo was standing, arms waving overhead so I wouldn't miss my stop this time. (She had also informed the bus company that there was an American on board who, like a child, needed to be told when to get off the bus). From there we drove a half-hour to Lake Ahvenlampi, jumped in a skiff and headed to a small island in the middle of a large lake. It was official. I was in the middle of nowhere.

But this was a very pretty nowhere. The summertime Lapland cottage is in pristine Arctic wilderness, set back on the land, well hidden in the trees so you can see the lake, but passing boaters can't really see you. The boat dock is the perfect place to enjoy the sunshine and big-sky sunsets.

The compact cottage is perfect too. And off the grid, with solar power for electricity, a wood-burning stove for heat, and a modern composting system. With no indoor plumbing, we used a rather luxurious outhouse: a prettily painted hut disguising the toilet and excrement beneath. After completing our business, we'd toss in a few wood chips to help sweeten the air. We used lake water to wash dishes and clothes and ourselves. Only drinking water is brought in from town.

The cottage was built in winter, when all building materials could be brought in by snow mobiles, hauling heavy equipment and supplies across the frozen-solid lake. The cottage complex features a one-room cabin with a living room, sleeping alcove, and step-in kitchen. Other buildings include a separate sleeping cottage, the prim outhouse, and of course, the sauna, the first building erected. This was Finland after all.

In Finland, sauna is not only a national pastime, it's an art. Almost every family has a sauna in their home and most Finns take a sauna every day, at least once a day. The temperature in the sauna is about 200° F (90° C.) After a sauna, most people stand in a wood-paneled steam room and bathe, washing with water warmed by the hot stones.

Since I'm North American, Pirjo introduced the idea of sauna to me in three stages:

The Towel: Each person has a small towel which they use to sit on while in the sauna. Because you enjoy the steam room naked, the towel helps maintain hygiene standards. This makes perfect sense to me.

Nudity: Because I was a little unsure of the whole ritual the first night, we waited until the second night to discard our clothes. That way when I ran naked into the water I knew exactly which direction to go. Usually we stayed in the steam room for about thirty minutes, throwing water on the hot coals to elicit more and more steam. Once we got a good sweat going, we ran down to the freezing cold lake and jumped it. It was quite a shock to the system.

Birch Branches: Birch branches were drying in the sauna the first night, giving off a wonderful aroma in the steam. By the third night, we were ready to put the branches to use. We took a freshly cut bunch of stems and hit our bodies with the foliage, creating a loud slapping noise. I'm still not entirely sure why we did this, although I think it has something to do with increasing circulation.

After my three-day indoctrination, I became quite a fan of the sauna. There's nothing more relaxing then ending your stressful day (OK, maybe my days in Lapland weren't so stressful, but I did do a lot of hiking and kayaking), in a warm steamy environment. I'm now one step closer to being Finnish!

I stayed at the idyllic cottage about ten days, with a couple of days in the middle spent hiking even further into the Arctic wilderness. Because we met hiking in the Himalayas, Pirjo assumed that I wanted to continue exploring the rugged outdoors (when I really just wanted to stay and sauna all day.)

So we headed even further north, to explore one of Finland's national parks: Urho Kekkonen National Park. Each day we hiked for about six hours and slept in huts strategically positioned throughout the park for trekkers. Each hut has sleeping capacity for ten people and a wood-burning stove, along with a gas stove and cooking equipment. We only had to pack sleeping bags, spare clothes and food.

One of my favorite Finnish treats is blueberry soup, which is quite tasty. While camping we mixed it with our porridge in the morning.

I saw other hikers drinking the hot bubbly blue soup from thermoses during an afternoon break.

Another Finn favorite is cloudberries. In fact, they can get a little crazy about them, carefully guarding the best spots for picking even from their best friends. During the month of August, Finns brave the mosquito-ridden lowlands to fill their buckets. We went out gathering one day and came back with three berries. Not quite worth the effort if you ask me, but then again, I'm not Finnish.

All in all, the Finns are a fairly rugged people. Our short expedition in the national park included lots of wood chopping, compass navigation in the fog, and fording frigid rivers, ice chips swirling in the water around our legs.

While none of the rivers we crossed had bridges, some had strategically placed logs to help us cross. At one point Pirjo stripped to her underwear, backpack held high over her head, and crossed in freezing water high up above her waist. Since I'm almost a full foot shorter, I elected to keep searching for a shallower crossing and was relieved to finally find one.

The wilderness scenery was beautiful, justifying all that exertion. But after several days of hiking and camping in the cold, we headed to the town of Inari (back again!), a deep 300 miles (482 km) into the Arctic Circle. We treated ourselves to a hotel, hot showers, and an impressive reindeer dinner. It was here in Inari that I had the opportunity to explore a completely new culture at

Siida, The National Museum of the Finnish Sámi.

The Sámi people are the indigenous people inhabiting the Arctic area, a swathe of land about the size of Sweden, encompassing the northern bits of Norway, Sweden, Finland, and Russia's Kola Peninsula. While the Sámi have been living in Lapland for more than 5,000 years, today there are less than 250,000 people claiming Sámi heritage. Most live in Norway, although the second largest population lives in the U.S. There are about 10,000 Sámi living in Finland.

Traditionally, the Sámi lived a semi-nomadic life, following the migration of the reindeer herds. They also engaged in coastal fishing, fur trapping, and sheep herding. Their traditional housing was an easily movable tee-pee-like dwelling called a *kota*.

After centuries of institutional discrimination, today the Sámi are most threatened by the urbanization of their culture, as well as environmental threats to their land, including oil exploration, mining, dam building, and logging. Climate change is also eroding the Sámi's traditional way of life and sacred Sámi sites are being used by the Norwegian and Swedish military as bomb practice ranges. I was touched by the plight of these nomadic people and all they had lost.

The Sámi are now formally protected under the *1966 U.N. Covenant on Civil and Political Rights* and they have won several cases brought before the U.N. Human Rights Committee. Each of the Nordic countries, plus Russia, have laws that explicitly protect Sámi rights and, in 1992, the Sámi were granted permission to use their language in schools.

Before my trip to Finnish Lapland I had never heard of the Sámi people, never hunted for cloudberries nor eaten reindeer, never taken a proper Finnish sauna, never traveled to the Arctic Circle.

These experiences all came to me because I made friends with a woman while hiking the Himalayas in far-off Nepal, where she was volunteering helping medical teams treat leprosy patients and I was volunteering at a home for abandoned children.

This, in a nutshell, is the essence of travel and exploration that I am so grateful for—the opportunity to wander the globe and open up my mind and heart to worlds I never knew existed.

Antoinette – Buenos Aires, Argentina

I first met Antoinette staying at a hostel in the heart of Buenos Aires. She had just arrived from volunteering in Lima, Peru and was struggling to make a connection with the city.

Buenos Aires is one of the most romantic, beautiful cities in all of Latin America, offering an intoxicating mix of old-world European architecture, funky graffiti-clad neighborhoods, high-end shopping, and copious amounts of delectable food and wine. Everyone loves Buenos Aires.

Everyone except Antoinette. She knew she should like it. She was trying to appreciate it. But no. The city just wasn't happening for her. So we sat in the hostel's communal living room dissecting her dislike.

I was trying to tell her that sometimes it takes a while for a city to grow on you. I shared my stories of not feeling the pulse of Bangkok, another of the world's great cities, until my third visit. It can't always be love at first city sight.

Antoinette and I had plenty in common. Like me and Pirjo, she's a serial volunteer, traveling at least once a year to donate her skills abroad. In fact, she's recently decided to give up her full-time job and launch a round-the-world trip of her own. As a pediatric operating room nurse, there are many in need of her talents. While in South America, she had just wrapped up a volunteer gig with **Heart Care International**, a nonprofit that provides life-saving heart surgeries for children who live in developing countries in Central and South America.

The organization was started more than 20 years ago by a New York City doctor who brought a group of his medical colleagues down to Guatemala to administer life-saving surgery for 25 Guatemalan children. To date, Heart Care International has helped pay for and perform more than 600 open heart surgeries, 175 interventional heart procedures, and 1,500 medical screenings for children and young adults.

And they don't just perform free operations for sick children. They help train local medical personnel to care for the patients and remain in close communication after the surgical team departs the host country to assist as medical issues arise.

If a child needs a surgery that cannot be performed abroad, Heart Care International can also help arrange for the patient (and a parent) to travel to the U.S. to receive medical attention. Heart Care also transports much needed medical supplies to host countries on every trip.

Antoinette was so passionate about her volunteer work that she infected me with her enthusiasm. I wanted to help children receive life-saving operations too! Since I don't have any medical skills to offer, I had the choice to volunteer as an administrative team member, source donated medical supplies, or make a donation.

I opted to make a donation to pay for a child's operation. This was one of the last donations of my trip and I made it in time for the holidays. A gift for a family with a sick child, and a gift for me. I felt so happy that I was able to make a significant contribution. I was grateful to think that I would be making a difference in that child's life.

As an Adventure Philanthropist, I felt I was just returning the favor, since I met lots of children during the course of my travels who made a difference in my life. I sang with children in Fiji, laughed until I cried with children in Ethiopia, and danced with toddlers high in the Himalayas. I've been lucky to have been graced by scores of lovely smiles.

I especially felt a lot of affection and an unexpected connection with a little known community known as the Kuna, who live in the San Blas islands. This tiny territory has a population of about 50,000 living in islands dotting Panama's Caribbean coast.

The Kuna, originally from Colombia, migrated north to the islands and Panamanian coastline in the 16th century. They lived happily until the 20th century when the Panamanian government tried to assimilate the Kuna, who fiercely resisted. The Kuna won and were granted an autonomous state, the Kuna Yala, in 1925. Today the Kuna Yala have the largest degree of autonomy of any South American indigenous people.

Traditionally, Kuna are a matrilineal society. The groom takes the last name of his bride, and he moves in with his wife's family after marriage. Kuna women are especially proud of their handicrafts, including the colorful *molas* that they hand embroider.

Molas are an art form, using the techniques of appliqué and reverse appliqué. Famous the world over, you see molas designs on wall hangings and pillow cases, as well as in multicolored patterns stitched in the panels of Kuna women's dresses. In fact the word "mola" means "clothing" in the Kuna language.

The Kuna are also known for the elaborate beadwork adorning their ankles and forearms. The bead pattern is held in place by a string that is wrapped around each individual bead. I bought an anklet and promptly lost the pattern for good. In the end, I simply knotted the strings on both ends and now wear the beads as a colorful necklace. Nice, but not only is the intricate design gone, but some of the significance for sure.

I got to visit the San Blas during a five-day sail from Cartagena, Colombia to Panama City. While bobbing at sea, the islanders often pulled alongside our catamaran to sell us lobster and fresh fruit. But one sparkling morning, we were invited to an island to have a meal prepared by the Kuna.

Lunch was a feast of coconut rice, fried chicken, lentils, and a salad. While it was freshly prepared, the cleanliness standards were a tad below what we're used to. I later learned that the spoon used to serve the rice was first washed in the bucket where pigs were drinking. It's no wonder a couple of us got sick.

Our hosts served us a lunch made especially for us tourists, since the Kuna diet is mainly fresh fish (instead of salad and lentils and chicken). In fact, the Kuna have almost no history of heart disease or cancer. Scientists believe their good health is not only attributed to diet, but also to the several cups of coca that they drink per day.

Interestingly, the Kuna have a very high incidence of albinism. The Kuna consider albinos to be a separate race of people and they are given a revered place in Kuna society. The pigmently-challenged are believed to have special powers and according to Kuna folklore they use these superhuman gifts to defend the moon against dragons. As such, the Kuna protect their sorcerers and only allow them to venture outside during a lunar eclipse.

During my visit, I saw several albino people, including small children (one had escaped and was running around outside!). I also saw an albino woman and her young daughter tucked away inside one of the huts. The little girl with white pigtails was sitting quietly on a small wooden stool. When I came to the door, I was invited in by her equally pale mother, who allowed me to give her daughter a coloring book and box of crayons.

The Kuna are a highly private people, so I was surprised to be invited in. They also intensely dislike having their photos taken, so I was again amazed that a young mother, swaying in a hammock, let me take a video of her breastfeeding and singing a lullaby to her baby.

I think I won this trust because when I arrived on the island, I sat with one of the families for a long while, talking (pantomiming) with the women. I also handed out stickers to the children and brought work books for the teachers to distribute at school. This is something I do quite often when travelling, bringing a supply of exercise books, pens, and pencils to share. I also like to bring a small treat for the children, usually stickers or crayons.

Since I knew ahead of time that I'd be visiting the islands, I stocked up on school supplies before departing Cartagena. The stickers I had found in a local dollar store were all forms of Smurfs and to my surprise the kids seemed to love them.

In fact, I was practically mobbed by screaming children. With a little help from my shipmates, we were able to form a line and allow each child to pick a sticker or two. Most of the kids wanted them placed directly on their bare chests, although a few goofballs fashioned Papa Smurf eye patches. The scary pirate-effect was somewhat diminished by the Smurfs' blinding blue bodies.

I spent only a few hours visiting the Kuna, but even in this short time, I was able to gain a better understanding of their culture and get a glimpse into their daily lives. I was also able to make one small friend, a little girl named Caroline.

Caroline was one of the first to receive a coloring book. She would quickly color a picture, then proudly show it to me. I would then point to a butterfly or a pair of Smurf shoes and name a color in Spanish and she would go away and return, coloring book in hand, with the picture complete. We replayed this light-hearted game throughout the duration of my visit.

It never ceases to amaze me how even though we come from vastly different cultures, we can still experience a meaningful exchange. Caroline was like any little kid anywhere, happy to receive an unexpected present and I was thrilled to share her happiness. I thank the Smurfs for that.

Yia – Sapa, Vietnam

I used to think that everyone living in Vietnam was Vietnamese, but the country is surprisingly ethnically diverse. The government recognizes fifty-four distinct groups, each with its own language, lifestyle, and cultural heritage.

About 12.7% of the Vietnamese population (more than 6 million people) claim minority tribe heritage. These tribes mainly live in the northern highland region. They benefit from relative independence and follow their own traditional customs and culture. For instance, religious practices among highland minorities tend to be rooted in animistic beliefs. I got to see some of these practices up close during my multi-day trek deep into the hills.

It was my thirty-six year old Hmong guide Yia, a mother of four, who introduced me to village life in Sapa. Even though she can't read or write, Yia is one savvy business woman. Her first language is Hmong, her second is English, and her third is Vietnamese (which is patchy). She learned English by selling handicraft souvenirs to tourists. Before Yia became a tour guide several years ago, she told me she had never walked more than three hours beyond her home village.

Throughout our hillside hike, we elected to take paths that were higher up the mountain where we saw few, if any, other tourists. This detour gave us plenty of time to talk about life in Yia's village. It also gave us the chance to meander and pick the leafy plants growing alongside our path. These greens were added to our stir-fried dinner of water buffalo meat that night. Pretty tasty.

Another guide, Sheng, also collected plants. She spent about a half-hour digging up roots that she later boiled and used to shampoo her hair. It was wonderful to see how these women still knew about the land and how to maximize the abundance that was around them.

When Yia invited us to her house for lunch, we couldn't help but notice a massive altar on the opposite wall of the main room, covered with paper images of chickens, pigs, and cows. There were also brightly painted red and gold paper, as well as some chicken feathers stuck about. Besides being a mountain guide, Yia and her husband are also local shamans.

I asked her if she sacrificed chickens on her altar and she nodded. She then went on to explain that when her fellow villagers are sick or scared or angry, she helps them feel better by sacrificing an animal (either real or paper). The live animal sacrifices are then eaten, while the paper sacrifices are either burned or cut to shreds. Yia confided that it was sometimes necessary to cut up images of people too.

Yia also showed us the indigo dying process used to make traditional Hmong clothing. Tunics are made out of hemp fabric that is then dyed and dried every single day for a minimum of three months. This laborious saturation process ensures the hemp fabric absorbs the dye and turns a dark, midnight blue color. The fabric is then rubbed with rocks to make it shiny.

Each tunic is then adorned with intricately needle-pointed arm bands and belts. These pieces of needlework take about a month to make and are a great source of pride for tribal women. In fact, when Hmong women greet one another, they often admire one another's outfit and compliment their choice of design. So familiar.

Each year Yia makes five sets of clothes for herself and her husband, three sets for her daughter, and two sets for her grandkids. The new clothes for the family are all ready in time for the New Year's celebration. I was especially lucky because Yia sold me one of her family's tunics (size XXL) and later I bought two hand-embroidered belts in the local Sapa village to go with it.

When I returned to Hanoi I tried on the tunic in front of a mirror and it looked fabulous! It was hard for me to see exactly what I was buying at the time because Yia's sister-in-law sold it to me while standing on the side of a mountain. The Hmong have a strange sense of timing when it comes to selling you things. They prefer to pounce on you while you're huffing up a steep mountain trail, trying to nab you when you're gasping for air and can't protest.

Hill tribes can act aggressive with tourists since the living conditions in highlands continues to lag behind that of urban Vietnamese. Minorities that live in the mountainous regions are known by a generic name Montagnards. (Although the Vietnamese often disparagingly call them "*moi*" meaning "savage.")

I was pleased to see that as Vietnam modernizes, it's making education a priority, even in the hill country. During my three-day excursion, I saw many new schools had been built during the last few years. We visited one school so we could watch Yia's daughter perform traditional Hmong dances in a recital celebrating the end of the school year. I too joined the celebration by making a small cash donation to the school and by passing out ballpoint pens to the children we met on the trail.

Trekking in Sapa was one of the most absorbing memories of my month-long trip to Vietnam and it was entirely due to Yia introducing me to her family and welcoming me into her home. Generous acts of hospitality like these never escape me. Being on the road for two years, I was always grateful for a home-cooked meal.

I was fortunate to have this gracious gesture repeated throughout my trip—in Beirut, Lebanon; Pokhara, Nepal; Copenhagen, Denmark; Cairo, Egypt; Kuala Lumpur, Malaysia; Roatan, Honduras; Dublin, Ireland; Livingston, Zambia; Tel Aviv, Israel; Bogota, Colombia, in the suburbs of Sydney, Australia, and throughout the United Kingdom, including the tiny Orkney Isle of Eday. And let's not forget my home-stay in Finnish Lapland and invitation to dine in the reed huts of my new-found friends in the San Blas Islands.

To me, this one act—opening up one's home—is the simplest and most direct way to express friendship and trust and respect. It's about sharing what you have and who you are.

I think this idea of someone sharing their home with me is especially poignant since I gave up my own home to travel the world. Not only did I elect to live out of a suitcase for the entire two years, but I launched this life of a nomad that I'm continuing to this day. The world has become my home.

The idea of home has yet another meaning for me. Before I left on my journey I was saving to buy a house. I didn't inherit a down payment and my family wasn't going to lend me one. I was a single working woman who was running a business and setting aside money every month to build my housing fund.

I had finally saved enough when I decided to take my hard-won savings and spend it on this trip. I decided I would not buy a house. I would travel the world instead.

Although it didn't register at the time, early on in my travels I made a $2,500 donation to *Gawad Kalinga*, a nonprofit based in the Philippines that provides for families living in poverty. My donation paid for a house. The house is in the neighborhood of Carmelray GK Village, Canlubang, Calamba City, Laguna. The owner is a Glenda, a thirty-eight year old woman and mother of two boys, Wilson and Ghio, ages twelve and thirteen.

So in the end I did buy a house. It just wasn't my house. It was a house for a family I have never met. A home for another single working woman, a mother, who would now be able to share it with the family she loved. I am eternally grateful to have had the opportunity to make her dream come true. And I'm thankful that I was able to make my dream of buying a house come true too.

Epilogue: THE AFTERMATH – COMING HOME

Upon returning home, I was impatient to discover the new me. For some reason, I thought that the change would be immediate once I stepped back onto U.S. soil. I would magically blossom into some other creature upon eating a French fry. But that didn't happen.

Instead, I was a little unsettled. Although in truth, after visiting 62 countries in 704 days, it would have been more surprising if I didn't feel somewhat dazed. But my discomfort was more than just a fish-out-of-water feeling.

First, there was the chronic sleep deprivation from years of sweating it out in jungle camps, swinging in hammocks with boa constrictors over my head, bedding down in bug-infested beach huts. But the real exhaustion came from never truly relaxing. As a solo female traveler, I needed to be vigilant for my safety, so I lived in a constant, if subtle, state of alert. I was mentally exhausted.

Second, I wasn't physically well. For about six months, I incorrectly thought my lack of energy and grumpy digestion was because I had decided to become a vegetarian. I thought my body wasn't getting the protein or iron or vitamins it needed. This wasn't the case. In fact, I had stomach problems and chronic fatigue.

My persistent Delhi-belly was caused by parasites I had picked up on the road. And not just one, but two. (Actually one parasite and one amoeba, but let's not split hairs.) These little intestinal intruders were ravishing my insides until I finally went to a doctor and was given a heavy dose of antibiotics to kill the critters. So it was a double whammy of physical ailments and emotional exhaustion.

This chronic stress was starting to take the form of frequent night sweats and panic attacks. While visiting with my friend Jenny, a trained psychologist, I was telling her about some of my distress. She suggested I might have a mild form of Post Traumatic Stress Disorder (PTSD). The "fight or flight" modus operandi that I'd been living under for two years causing far more mental strain than I had imagined.

On some level, I still had to process all that I had seen and done. As I began to unpack my memories, my anxiety further intensified. I struggled with digesting the immensity of what I had witnessed, my glimpses at people's lives and struggles. I became quieter. I tried to stay still. To absorb the enormity of it all.

At the beginning of the trip I was giddy with the possibilities of who I might become, how my travels might open up new dimensions within me. It never dawned on me that the person to emerge might be less effusive, less trusting of others, more circumspect. This was a depressing thought. No one wants to change for the worse. I left a carefree person and now I wasn't. If not exactly sad, I was definitely more somber.

In order to process my recollections, I decided on a memory regimen. I would approach my memories more sparingly, instead of trying to ingest them in one gulp. My plan is to take them off my memory shelf one at a time. In this way, I can more easily savor the good times and nibble on the bad.

Thankfully, this grazing approach has helped me to regain my balance. I am now sifting through all the emotions that I had absorbed deep inside. All the hopes and joys, all the pain and fear, all the awesome surprises. As memories unfold, my view shifts, and each time I have the opportunity to recognize, react, and relive.

Every now and then, I spare a moment to check in the mirror, and am relieved to recognize the image of the woman who left on her adventure more than two years ago. Except the person staring back at me now has a wider perspective and deeper understanding of humanity, both in the large macro sense and on a smaller, more intimate level.

Yes, I came back a fuller person. More complicated. Slightly conflicted. And calmer.

Mostly I returned home grateful. Oh so grateful to have had this experience of a lifetime and to be able to continually learn from it. This mental unfurling continues as I gently unwrap each memory, enjoying the gifts they present. Now, every day is just like Christmas.

Florida, October 2013

Index:
GLOBAL HUMANITARIAN ORGANIZATIONS

During my global trek, I supported a host of humanitarian organizations by volunteering, fostering dialogue around social issues, and making donations. The donations were facilitated via two channels:

GoErinGo! Fund is my personal charitable giving fund. Before I left on my journey, I made an initial $25,000 contribution to give away during my travels. As of October 2013, the fund has made 75 grants, totally more than $35,500. Of the grants, 70% went to fund projects overseas, with 30% funding programs in the U.S. A full listing of donations, including the date, name, sector, and amount of each donation, is on the www.GoErinGo.com website.

Donate My Dollars is a feature on the www.GoErinGo.com web site that encourages readers to join the fun of philanthropy by participating in directing GoErinGo! Fund charitable gifts. Nearly every month, readers vote on which organizations should receive donations and the amount of the grant. A special thanks to all GoErinGo readers who participated in this global outreach effort.

If you too would like to become more involved, I've included the contact details of the socially conscious businesses and nonprofit organizations mentioned within this book:

Animal Welfare

ALERT (African Lion & Environmental Research Trust) promotes responsible development in Zambia and Zimbabwe, working within communities to implement locally conceived and targeted solutions to preserve local lion populations. http://lionalert.org/page/about-us You can volunteer with ALERT via their for-profit sister company Lion Encounter. www.lionencounter.com

Elephant Village, situated near Luang Prabang, Laos, is a privately owned, for-profit elephant camp and tourist destination approved by the Lao government and operated by international specialists and volunteers who focus on the protection and rehabilitation of elephants in Laos. www.elephantvillage-laos.com

Kosgoda Sea Turtle Conservation Project is located on the west coast of Sri Lanka monitoring local sea turtle activity. In addition to a breeding program, they work with the community to help protect of marine reptile species. www.kosgodaseaturtle.org

Marina Megafauna Foundation was formed to research, protect, and conserve the large populations of marine megafauna found along the Mozambican coastline, such as sharks, rays, marine mammals, and turtles. A U.S. nonprofit, the main research facility is in Tofo, Mozambique. www.marinemegafauna.org

Sepilok Orang Utan Rehabilitation Centre is an orangutan rehabilitation project for orphaned baby orangutans rescued from logging sites, plantations, and illegal hunting. The sanctuary is located within the Kabili-Sepilok Forest Reserve in the state of Sabah, East Malaysia and is run by the Sabah Wildlife Department in conjunction with Orangutan Appeal UK, a UK charity. www.orangutan-appeal.org.uk

Arts & Culture

Cambodia's Land Mine Museum and Relief Center is a nonprofit run by Cambodians based in Siem Reap. More than a museum, it is also a home that provides education and support for dozens of at-risk youth and children affected by the threat of landmines. www.CambodiaLandmineMuseum.org

My Sisters' Kitchen is a program of Darwin Community Arts, a nonprofit based in Darwin, Australia. The program brings together recent refugees in a safe space where they can share recipes and stories as they create a new life in their adopted land. www.darwincommunityarts.org.au

Radio Musi-o-tunya, the "Smoke that Thunders," is a community radio station based in Livingstone, Zambia. Broadcasting in English, Silozi, and Chitonga, the nonprofit radio station serves as an outlet for political and cultural discourse throughout much of western Zambia. www.facebook.com/RadioMusiOTunya

Siida, The National Museum of the Finnish Sámi is located in Inari, Finland and is the national museum representing the spiritual and material culture of the Finnish Sámi. Its main purpose is to support the identity and cultural self-esteem of the Sámi people. www.siida. fi/contents/sami-museum

This is Baladi is a Beirut-based nonprofit that takes Lebanese school children on field trips. These excursions focus on the country's historical sites and diverse cultures, including food and the arts. Their goal is to build a new sentiment of empathy, solidarity, and national unity in post-conflict Lebanon. www.thisisbiladi.com

Tuol Sleng Genocide Museum, known as S-21, is a former torture and detention center. The historical site located in Phnom Penh is now a museum, serving as a testament to the crimes of the Khmer Rouge and as a memorial dedicated to its victims. www.lonelyplanet.com/cambodia/phnom-penh/sights/museum/tuol-sleng-museum

Children & Youth

ChildSafe Network is an international network based in Phnom Penh, Cambodia comprising local and international advocates that protect children, especially street children, from abuse. Businesses that support child safety in Southeast Asia sport the ChildSafe logo. www.childsafe-cambodia.org

ECPAT (End Child Prostitution and Trafficking) is a global network of organizations and individuals working together to eliminate child prostitution, child pornography, and the trafficking of children for sexual purposes. The nonprofit monitors a network of eighty-one local organizations in seventy-four countries. www. ecpat.net

Lotus Petals purchases bikes and repairs kits for Cambodian girls. By providing heavy-terrain bicycles to hundreds of at-risk and exploited girls, this nonprofit is helping to keep girls in school and to end the cycle of poverty in Cambodia and other Southeast Asian countries. www.globalgiving.org/projects/lotuspedals

Education & Job Training

Big Brother Mouse, a Lao-run nonprofit based in Luang Prabang, publishes high-quality books in the local language. They encourage Laotians to read through a series of book parties, village reading rooms, teacher trainings, language classes, and reading workshops. www.bigbrothermouse.com

The Book Bus, a charity registered in England and Wales, aims to improve child literacy rates in Africa, Asia, and South America by providing children with books and the inspiration to read them. The group hosts volunteers in Zambia, Malawi, India, and Ecuador. www.thebookbus.org

Empowering Women of Nepal (EWN) is a Nepali nonprofit based in Pokhara that trains disadvantaged Nepali women to be trekking guides. EWN graduates are often offered a paid apprenticeship training program through the for-profit trekking company 3Sisters Trekking. www.3sistersadventuretrek.com/sisters/ewn

Phare Ponleu Selpak, "The Brightness of Art," is a cultural organization in Battambang, Cambodia, that offers young people a way out of poverty by training them to become professional artists and performers. Its internationally recognized circus highlights social issues affecting the children. www.phareps.org

Youth Community Training Center, located in Livingstone, Zambia, offers vocational training in tailoring, knitting, catering, carpentry, plumbing, and bricklaying. The Center is.run by the local Catholic Diocese in coordination with CeLim, an Italian nonprofit overseeing development projects in Zambia and throughout Sub-Saharan Africa. www.olgasproject.com/yctc_uk.htm

Crazy Kim's, in the Vietnamese city of Nha Trang, is a free school run out of the bar Crazy Kim's. The organization helps disadvantaged teenagers and young adults learn English and computer skills. www. crazykimvietnam.wordpress.com/school

Environment

Antarctica Site Inventory is a program run by the U.S.-based nonprofit Oceanites, which is dedicated to scientific exploration and conservation of the Antarctic region. The organization is funded by many of the signers of the Antarctic Treaty governments, including the U.S., UK, and Germany. www.oceanites.org

Guaruma is a local Honduran nonprofit that teaches the youth of the Cangrejal River Valley about eco-tourism, conservation, and environmental issues. By providing after-school classes and ecotourism services, the group seeks to promote rural community development and lasting changes in attitudes. www.guaruma.org

Heart of Borneo Rainforest Foundation is an international campaign that asks companies that import timber and palm oil from Borneo to only buy goods that are from sustainable sources. As part of this project, all 3 of the island's governments (Brunei, Indonesia and

Malaysia) committed to protect, manage, and restore 220,000 km of forests. www.heartofborneo.org

Jatun Sacha Foundation is an Ecuadorian non-governmental organization dedicated to the conservation, investigation, and management of ecologically important habitats in Ecuador. They place volunteers in their biological stations and provide field experience in environmental education, wildlife conservation, sustainable aquaculture, and scientific research. www.jatunsacha.org/ingles

Roatan Marine Park is a community-based nonprofit located on the island of Roatan, Honduras. The organization is dedicated to enforcing Honduran environmental protection laws and promoting the conservation of Roatan's coastal and marine resources. www.roatanmarinepark.com

Scuba Junkie is a for-profit dive resort located on the island of Borneo, Sabah, Malaysia. The resort is eco-friendly, featuring green waste systems, solar energy, and using only biodegradable cleaning products and plastics. They also offer a slate of environmental projects for volunteers. www.scubajunkiekk.com

Sustainable Bolivia is a nonprofit based in Cochabamba, Bolivia, providing Bolivian organizations with much needed human and financial resources while giving international students the opportunity to gain practical work experience through internships and volunteer opportunities. www.sustainablebolivia.org

Health

The Birthing Project USA provides pre-natal and neo-natal care for African America women in the United States, helping to encourage better birth outcomes. The nonprofit organization also assists Garifuna women living in Honduras, women in rural Malawi, and mothers-to-be in Cuba. www.birthingprojectusa.org

First Garifuna Hospital, the only free hospital in Honduras, provides healthcare to isolated Garifuna communities. The hospital is supported, in part, by the California Honduras Institute for Medical and Educational Support (CHIMES) Project, a nonprofit based in Sacramento, California. www.chimesproject.org

Heart Care International is a U.S. nonprofit providing high quality and compassionate surgical and medical care pro bono to needy children and young adults with heart disease in developing countries. They work in Guatemala, the Dominican Republic, El Salvador, and Peru. www.heartcareintl.org

St. Joseph's Hospice is located in Livingstone, Zambia. Part of the Catholic Diocese of Livingstone, the hospice provides care to people with disabilities and those living with HIV /AIDS, TB, and malaria. www.dioceseoflivingstone.blogspot.com/p/institutions

The Leprosy Mission International (TLMI), founded in 1874, is the oldest and largest leprosy-focused organization in the world today. Based in the UK, TLMI directly supports 200 leprosy projects in 26 countries and furnishes financial and project support in another 24 countries. www.leprosymission.org

Housing & Human Services

APOPO researches, develops, and implements detection-rat (HeroRATS) technology for humanitarian purposes such as Mine Action and Tuberculosis detection. A Belgian nonprofit, its headquarters is in Tanzania, with operations in Mozambique, Thailand, Angola, and Cambodia. www.apopo.org/en

Gawad Kalinga is a nonprofit based in the Philippines that is dedicated to ending poverty for 5 million Filipino families by 2024 by providing housing and food welfare programs, as well as community building projects. GK1World is a U.S. nonprofit supporting the work of Gawad Kalinga. www.gk1world.com

Ghar Sita Mutu, "House with Heart," provides a safe home for abandoned children, a training center for destitute women, and an outreach program for needy families in Kathmandu, Nepal. The organization is a Nepali non-profit. www.housewithaheart.org

Hagar Cambodia is an organization registered in Switzerland that operates commercial and non-profit entities and engages in private and public sector partnerships supporting women and child victims of trafficking, domestic violence, and exploitation in Cambodia. www.hagarinternational.org

Little Angels Needy Children and Orphans cares for 200 children with the aim of promoting their well-being in the Bufuka area on Lake Bunyonyi, Uganda. *For more information, please contact me at Erin@GoErinGo.com before contributing to this organization. www.littleangelsuganda.org

Lubashi Home provides residential care for orphans and vulnerable children in Livingstone, Zambia. The home cares for about 50 children, aged between 5 and 10 years, most of them orphaned as a result of the AIDS pandemic, which affects about 30% of adults in Livingstone. www.lubasihome.org

Lushomo Home is a residential care facility in Livingstone, Zambia for young girls, aged between 10 and 17 years, who have suffered abuse from family members or friends. The home provides a safe place for the girls to live and pursue their education. www.spreadhealth.org

Singithi Sevana, meaning "Children's Rest," is a state-registered children's home in Kandy, Sri Lanka providing residential care for orphaned and needy children, aged between 2 and 12 years. The home cares for 32 children, offering them an uninterrupted secondary school education. www.SingithiSevana.org

Trailblazer Foundation is a U.S.-based nonprofit working in Siem Reap, Cambodia seeking to foster healthy families, provide sufficient food, and encourage sustainable incomes. Trailblazer works in rural villags funding water projects, building schools, and by investing in other community development programs. www.thetrailblazerfoundation.org

Social Justice

International Campaign for Tibet was founded 25 years ago and is based in the U.S., with offices in Europe and Australia. It advocates for the rights of Tibetan people. The organization works with and is guided by His Holiness the Dalai Lama. www.savetibet.org

Egyptian Center for Women's Rights (ECWR) is an independent, non-partisan, and non-governmental organization committed to supporting the political and the legal status of women in Egypt. Based in Cairo, ECWR works to eliminate all forms of discrimination and establish gender equality. www.ecwronline.org

Ethiopian Women Lawyers Association is a non-profit, non-partisan, and voluntary association founded by a group of Ethiopian women lawyers to promote the legal, economic, social, and political status of Ethiopian women. Based in Addis Ababa, they seek to end discrimination and ensure the equal treatment of Ethiopian women. www.everythingaddis.com/ethiopian-women-lawyers-association

National Network of Positive Women Ethiopia is a non-profit, non-political, and secular national network of associations of HIV Positive Women Ethiopians. The group supports the formation and functioning of sixteen positive women associations and regional networks across Ethiopia. www.nnpwe.org

SlutWalks is a worldwide movement calling for an end to rape culture by challenging the mindsets and stereotypes of victim-blaming in cases of rape. Participants protest on the streets against explaining or excusing rape by referring to any aspect of a woman's appearance. www.facebook.com/SlutWalk

UN Trust to End Violence Against Women is a global grant-making mechanism exclusively dedicated to addressing violence against women and girls in all its forms. Established by the United Nations General Assembly, the trust has delivered more than $86 million to 351 initiatives in 128 countries and territories. www.unwomen.org

Women & Girls

El HaLev, meaning "To the Heart," is an Israeli nonprofit that effects social change by empowering and reducing violence against women, teens, children, seniors, and people with special needs through teaching martial arts and self-defense training. www.elhalev.org

HarassMap is a project based in Cairo that seeks to end the social acceptability of sexual harassment in Egypt by using technology. The online reporting system acts as an advocacy, prevention, and response tool, highlighting the severity and pervasiveness of the sexual harassment in the country. www.HarassMap.org

IMPACT is a personal safety, assertiveness, and self-defense training program for women. It is part of a comprehensive effort to prevent sexual assault, acts of interpersonal violence, and boundary violations. The organization has eleven chapters in the U.S., as well as chapters in Israel and the UK. www.impactselfdefense.org

About the Author

A former finance executive, Erin Michelson is a consultant specializing in asset generation and expansion strategies for nonprofit organizations. She has worked on every side of philanthropy: holding management positions with several leading organizations, founding her own nonprofit, serving as a Board of Director, and running her own charitable fund.

A recognized social entrepreneur and recipient of multiple international awards, Erin has lived and studied in Auckland, Beijing, and Cape Town. She holds degrees in International Relations, Political Science, and Government & Public Administration. Visit her website at www.GoErinGo.com.